BE YOUR OWN
COMPANY
SECRETARY

SECOND EDITION

A J SCRINE

KOGAN
PAGE

Copyright © A J Scrine 1987, 1990

All rights reserved
First published in Great Britain in 1987 by
Kogan Page Limited, 120 Pentonville Road,
London N1 9JN. Reprinted 1988, 1989.
Second edition 1990.

British Library Cataloguing in Publication Data

A CIP record for this book is available from the British Library.

ISBN 0-7494-0364-0
ISBN 0-7494-0260-1 Pbk

Typeset by The Castlefield Press Limited, Wellingborough, Northants in
Palatino 10/11.5 pt.

Printed and bound in Great Britain by Biddles Limited, Guildford

Contents

Introduction   **7**

1. What is a Company Secretary?   **9**

2. Limited Liability Companies – What Are They?   **10**
A company 10; Directors 13; The Registrar of Companies 13

3. How to Set Up a Company   **15**
Buying a company 15; What you receive 17

4. Ready to Start   **22**
Directors 22; Secretary 30; Subscribers' shares 32;
The registered office 33; Stationery 36; Use of a business
name 37; Company seal 37; Accounting reference date 37;
Auditor 38; Opening a bank account 39

5. Running the Company   **40**
Board meetings 40; Minutes 48; Writing up the statutory
books and statutory returns 51

6. The Continuing Routines   **54**
Statutory books and returns 54; Board meetings 55;
General meetings 56

7. Year-end Duties   **63**
The annual tasks 63; The Directors' Report 64;
Annual accounts 68; Dispensing with laying accounts 69;
Annual General Meeting 69; The Annual Return 72

8. Special Events   **73**
Shares 73; Changes of director and/or secretary 80;
Dividends 80; Registration of charges 81; Change of
company name 83; Alteration of Memorandum and
Articles of Association 83; Sealing of documents 85;
Increase of authorised capital 86; Issue of shares 86;
Terminating the appointment of a director 91; Change of
auditors 92; Nominee shareholdings in subsidiary
companies 93

9. *Terminating a Company*   **96**

Appendix   **97**
Commonly Used Company Forms

Bibliography   **110**

Index   **111**

Introduction

The increasing complexities of the law confronting the businessman are well known and there are many specialised publications dealing with various aspects. This guide will deal with only one particular aspect of business law which has become more important recently: this is the area known as company secretarial practice. With the continued growth in the number of limited companies registered under the Companies Acts, as indicated in the figures published annually by the Registrar of Companies (which show that there are now some 1,112,000 limited companies in existence) and general concern over the failure of many companies to comply with the statutory requirements to the detriment of creditors, shareholders and the public, it seems timely to produce a practical work for the guidance of the directors and secretary of the small private company who do not hold a relevant professional qualification. The work will also be of value to students of various professional bodies whose examination syllabuses include some or all aspects of company law and to those who are involved with non-trading concerns which operate for convenience through the vehicle of a limited company. These may include residents' associations looking after maintenance and security matters for blocks of flats, small partnerships, and perhaps small charities and co-operative bodies whose affairs are dealt with by a company. There are probably many people responsible to some extent for such companies who may be unfamiliar with the requirements of company law and particularly the formal duties of keeping the statutory books and making out statutory forms which have to be sent to the Registrar of Companies on the occurrence of certain events. Failure to comply with such requirements can of course lead to penalties and, as has been said in other contexts, 'ignorance of the law is no excuse'.

The book also describes procedures which the secretary of a

company should ensure are carried out during the course of each year and this may help to make sure that these matters are not overlooked. Some of the procedures, eg arranging the meetings and writing the minutes, are also relevant to those connected with small voluntary social and charitable organisations which frequently tend to operate by means of an executive or similar committee, which is much like a board of directors.

The areas for which a company secretary has a statutory duty are outlined. No prior knowledge of the subject is assumed and the book does not set out to provide much detail on the more intricate matters; it is essentially practical, to cover the normal events in the company's life which involve compliance with statutory requirements. It is not a complete reference work for all aspects of company law and when users of this guide meet a situation or event which is not mentioned, they should consult a professional adviser – a chartered secretary, chartered accountant or lawyer.

The contents are based on situations encountered in the practical experience of the author over a number of years as a company secretary. It should perhaps be stressed that the role of the secretary is not that of a stuffy bureaucrat but of a contributor to the successful operation of the enterprise by ensuring that the administrative wheels in the organisation run smoothly.

Those who are already involved in running a company will find the material from Chapter 4 onwards of particular value.

A short bibliography is given at the end of the book and further advice may be obtained from professional advisers.

The author would like to record his thanks to the Institute of Chartered Accountants in England and Wales, the Institute of Chartered Secretaries and Administrators, the Registrar of Companies and many colleagues whose help and advice have been invaluable. He hopes that users running their own small companies will find the book a useful and practical guide to most of the routine and recurring duties of the directors and the secretary.

CHAPTER 1

What is a Company Secretary?

Every limited company is required by the Companies Acts to have at least one director and a secretary, sometimes called the company secretary. These two positions may not be held by one person, unless there is also at least one other director. The secretary has responsibilities to the directors, the shareholders and the company, as well as to certain third parties such as the Registrar of Companies.

The secretary is responsible for providing a service to the directors, both formally by convening board meetings as required and writing and keeping the minutes of those meetings, and by doing all he can to enable the board to function properly and in accordance with the law. He is usually expected to have some knowledge of a number of legal matters and to be able to advise the board on these.

The secretary is usually responsible for dealing with the shareholders. This involves convening meetings for them, as well as processing transfers of shares and paying dividends.

Another task of the secretary is often to be the chief administrative officer of the company and he is frequently responsible for keeping the accounts, negotiating contracts, attending to insurances, pension schemes and possibly trademark and patent affairs. He may also look after personnel matters. By reason of his office he has authority to commit the company to third parties in many matters.

The Companies Acts require all companies to maintain a series of formal records, known as statutory books. One of the particular responsibilities of the secretary is to keep these books and to send forms and returns giving information about the company to an official of the Department of Trade and Industry called the Registrar of Companies.

In summary, therefore, the secretary provides the company with a general administration service and should perform many duties which are ancillary to, but essential for, its efficient operation.

9

CHAPTER 2

Limited Liability Companies – What Are They?

The reader may well be unfamiliar with the concept of limited liability companies and the roles of the directors and the secretary: these are therefore described here in general terms.

A company

There are many kinds of organisation which can be adopted for a business operation. These include:

an unincorporated concern, such as
   a sole trader;
   a partnership;
(both of these trade under their own name and responsibility; the owners carry personal liability for the business);

a limited company, either
   a private company, or
   a public company;
(these are limited either by shares or, in the case of a few private companies, by guarantee (charities, for example); the owners' liability is limited);

a chartered company;
(one which was given a Royal Charter many years ago)

an unlimited company;
(an example is a learned society)

a friendly society;
(an example is a trade union).

The last three kinds of company are unusual. Apart from sole traders and partnerships, the most common type of business organisation is the company limited by shares, either private or public. A limited company requires a company secretary as well as directors because of the requirements of the Companies Acts.

A working definition of a limited company is that it is a legal entity which has contractual powers – that is, it has the advantage of being able to do things in its own right and under its own name. A company is a means by which individuals can pool their resources to provide the assets for a business which will be carried on in its own right. The contributions become shares when the legal entity is created by incorporation as a limited company, and share certificates are issued as documents of title to those who have contributed resources (which may be money or other assets) and these people are called the members. Thus this form of association enables individuals to work together by investing in shares in the company which then operates as a business.

This books deals with companies limited by shares. Such companies are created under the Companies Acts which establish the legal framework within which they are formed and operate. They are, consequently, subject to a considerable amount of statutory regulation, including a requirement to maintain a record of certain information relating to the company at a central Registry administered by the Registrar of Companies (see page 13).

Limited companies are divided into two classes – private and public. Broadly speaking, a public company is one whose shares are available to the general public through the Stock Exchange; it may be recognised from the inclusion in its name of either the words public limited company or the abbreviation plc.

Any company limited by shares which does not fall within this description is a private company. Public companies (and their subsidiaries, which are usually private companies) are not dealt with further in this book. Here we deal only with the regulations relating to company secretarial practice in independent private companies.

A private company is generally owned by a few people (the shareholders or members) and is in a small way of business. There must be at least two members of a company (there is no maximum number) and these own the shares in the company and have the right of voting at general meetings when the elections of directors and auditor and certain other matters are decided. They are entitled to share in profits (by dividend) and assets (on liquidation). If the business grows it can continue as a private company, but if it is desired to raise extra capital, or the owners wish to realise the value of their investment, they can bring in additional shareholders by offering the shares to the public at large (as distinct from offering shares privately to their friends), and it has to become a public company. It is a criminal offence to offer shares in a private company to the public at large, though there are some exceptions to this – for example, offers to existing members or to employees. Many quite large businesses are private companies, however, and there is no reason why they should not remain so, provided the existing shareholders are quite happy to carry on holding all the shares and do not want to be able to realise the capital value of those shares by selling them to someone else at any time.

A limited company has the major advantage of limited liability, which means that those individuals who have put their capital into the business by subscribing for the shares are not liable for the company's debts beyond the amount they have subscribed (provided there has been no fraud, deceit or other malpractice). Thus, when a company is set up as a limited liability company the shareholders' personal assets are kept separate from their business assets. If the business cannot meet its liabilities creditors then have recourse only to the business assets, and shareholders are liable only for the amount they have already subscribed or have agreed to subscribe for their shares. In practice, directors and shareholders in small companies may have to provide personal guarantees or security for some purposes, for example bank loans, but this does not usually apply to trading debts.

Another advantage of a limited company is that it is easy to transfer ownership, or part ownership, of the company by selling some or all of the shares, or to allow another individual to invest in the business by issuing new shares. The change of ownership can take place without disturbing the operation of the business. The company can enter into contracts, for example leases or trading contracts, in its own name. It does not have to be wound up when there is a change or death among the shareholders or directors (unlike a partnership which may terminate if there is a change of partner, although a new one will usually be formed immediately).

The treatment of a company for tax purposes differs in some respects from that of a sole trader or partnership. The profits can to some extent be held within the company rather than go directly to its shareholders. If profits are high in one year the sole trader might pay a high rate of income tax. In a limited company the directors can be paid an annual remuneration to spread their income more evenly over the following years. This is not dealt with in detail here and readers should contact an accountant for further advice.

Directors

The directors are the persons who are entrusted with the task of managing the company, and of running the business, because of course the company cannot act by itself as it is an impersonal entity. The directors are appointed or elected by the shareholders and their duties, responsibilities and liabilities are either expressly stated in the Companies Acts or are necessarily implied in considerable detail in that part of the Acts known as Table A (which is explained on page 20). This states that 'the business of the company shall be managed by the directors who may exercise all the powers of the company'. A private company must have at least one director and frequently the minimum and perhaps the maximum number of directors is laid down in the Articles of Association. It is necessary to maintain records of the directors of the company which include a number of items of personal information. When the directors are acting or meeting as a body they are generally referred to as the Board.

If there is only one director he or she is not permitted to be also the secretary but if there are two or more directors the offices of director and secretary may be combined by one of them.

The Registrar of Companies

It is convenient at this point to introduce the Registrar of Companies. The Registrar is a public official appointed by the Secretary of State for Trade and Industry.

The duties of the Registrar are to administer the regulatory aspects of the Companies Acts, primarily by maintaining records of all companies. This means being responsible for ensuring that all the statutory requirements relating to the formation of every new company have been complied with, issuing the Certificate of Incorporation, and then receiving the various statutory returns which have to be submitted on behalf of all the companies. These returns are filed and may be inspected (or searched) by any person on payment of a small fee, either in person at the appropriate office or by post. There are also a number of company agents (mentioned on page 15 in connection with the formation of companies) who will carry out searches for an applicant.

All enquiries relating to the registration of companies having their registered offices in England and Wales should be addressed to:

The Registrar of Companies, Companies House, Crown Way, Maindy, Cardiff CF4 3UZ (tel 0222 388588).

Company records can be inspected at this address and at the London Search Room:

Companies House, 55–71 City Road, London EC1Y 1BB (tel 071–253 9393).

Enquiries relating to companies having their registered offices in Scotland should be addressed to:

The Registrar of Companies, Exchequer Chambers, 102 George Street, Edinburgh EH2 3DJ (tel 031–226 5774).

Generally speaking the law in Scotland applicable to companies is the same as the law in England, though there are some differences in general law which do not concern us here.

Northern Ireland has its own entirely separate Companies Acts and all enquiries about companies registered there should be addressed to:

The Registrar of Companies, Department of Commerce, 43–47 Chichester Street, Belfast BT1 4RJ (tel 0232 234121).

The particular requirements relating to Northern Ireland companies are not referred to here, though many aspects of company secretarial practice follow English practice fairly closely.

CHAPTER 3

How to Set Up a Company

It is possible to take all the necessary steps to form a company yourself, but this is not a practical proposition for the inexperienced. Anyone setting up a business needs a clear knowledge of the kind of business which the company is to carry on, who is to run it and what they want to call it.

In practice if you wish to run your business as a limited company it is usually best to approach one of the specialised company formation agents (who advertise widely), and purchase a company. This company may be one which the agent has already formed or it may be formed specially for you. The agent will advise which alternative is best and help you obtain what you require.

Buying a company

The procedure for buying a company is simple. The work needed to form the company is done by the company formation agent. A ready-formed company might be purchased from the agent, and the Memorandum and Articles of Association altered as necessary (these are explained on pages 17–20). Such a company is often called an 'off-the-shelf' company. In other cases, you will choose the name and nature of the business first and then pass these details to the agent who will proceed to form the company in accordance with your requirements. The cost of acquiring a company will vary slightly but is approximately £125 at the time of writing. Advertisements by company formation agents are found in many business publications, or information may be obtained from a solicitor, accountant, bank manager or other professional adviser.

The contents of the Memorandum and Articles must be agreed and the name of the company chosen. The names of the first director(s), the secretary and the subscribers for the first two shares

15

in the company (See Chapter 4 page 22) and the Registered Office address must also be decided. If an off-the-shelf company is purchased these details will already have been settled by the agent, but they may have to be changed after the purchase is completed.

The name must be acceptable to the Registrar, who has issued *Notes for Guidance of Registered Companies*. It can be chosen fairly freely, though there are some words which are prohibited except in certain circumstances – for example the words 'bank', 'royal' or 'international' – to prevent companies appearing to have greater funding or presence than is the case and to protect existing organisations.

The other, and perhaps more important constraint on the choice of a name for the new company, is that it should not be the same as, or very similar to, that of an existing company. This can be checked by looking at the index of company names maintained by the Registrar of Companies at Companies House in Cardiff or London, or in Edinburgh if the company is to be formed in Scotland. The name selected must include 'Limited' as the last word.

The Memorandum and Articles of Association and other documents then have to be lodged with the Registrar of Companies (this will be done by the company formation agent) with the requisite fee. Provided all is in order the Registrar will issue the Certificate of Incorporation which certifies that the legal requirements have been fulfilled. From the date on which this Certificate is issued the company comes into existence as a corporate body and can begin trading immediately.

It is possible to buy a company which is already trading from the existing owner, who may perhaps be retiring. In this case the shares held by the present shareholders will be purchased and share transfer forms completed. There will usually be a purchase agreement as well, recording a number of matters such as the price, date of transfer, responsibility for past debtors and creditors and giving some warranties about the business. If this is how you acquire the company you should obtain the items mentioned below from the vendor in the same way as if the company had been purchased from a company formation agent, but there will, of course, be some entries in the statutory books already, and there may be copies of previous company forms and returns.

It may be that a new business is being started and the new company you have just bought will take all the action necessary to set up the business. On the other hand, the newly formed company will very often take over the existing business of a small trader, so the kind of business for which the company is needed is already decided. In this guide we have taken as a general example a small

shop – a confectioner, tobacconist and new agent,
whether the new company is taking over an
being formed for the purpose of setting u
essential company secretarial steps are the sar

What you receive

Once you have bought a company you will recei   wing
items from the company formation agent:

> Certificate of Incorporation
> Memorandum and Articles of Association
> statutory books
> company seal
> share certificates
> signed share transfer forms for the subscribers' shares (possibly)
> copies of any statutory forms which have already been lodged
>   with the Registrar of Companies
> letters of resignation of the first director and secretary (if an off-
>   the-shelf company)
> draft minutes of the first board meeting (usually)
> warranty that there are no undisclosed liabilities and that the
>   company has not previously traded (if an off-the-shelf
>   company).

These items will be described in turn.

Certificate of Incorporation
This is effectively a birth certificate for the company. It is issued by
the Registrar of Companies on receipt of all the necessary
documents and on his being satisfied that these and the proposed
name are in order. Once the Certificate of Incorporation has been
issued, the company is in being. The Certificate must be kept safely,
but it is not necessary to display it on the office wall (though you
may do so if you wish).

Memorandum and Articles of Association
A company is governed by its Memorandum and Articles of
Association. They are usually in one document, but we will look at
them separately here. A copy should be given to each director, but
copies are not usually given to shareholders; the company's bankers
and auditor will also require a copy. Very briefly, they are the
external face of the company (the Memorandum) and the internal
face of the company (the Articles).

randum of Association

ain function of the Memorandum is to state the purpose for
which the Company has been formed. It is divided into clauses.

The first clause will state the name of the company. The second
clause will state in which country the company is registered, which
governs where the registered office is situated – England and Wales,
Wales (if the company specially wishes to be Welsh) or Scotland.

The third clause – usually called the objects clause – states what
the company may do. Until recently a company could not carry on
any business not included in this clause which, therefore, usually
set out not only the main purpose of the company, for example to
carry on business as a confectioner, tobacconist and newsagent, but
also ancillary purposes which can and will need to be combined with
the main activity, such as to run a delivery service. If the
Memorandum states that the company has been established to buy
and sell confectionary then that is *all* it can do. It will not be able to
sell newspapers or stationery, nor could it borrow or lend money,
nor purchase or lease property. For this reason, the objects clause of
a company's Memorandum is usually worded widely to include
those ancillary purposes which experience has shown are needed in
addition to the main business activity to enable it to function
properly. The first paragraph of the third clause of the
Memorandum states the company's main object, followed by other
paragraphs setting out the ancillary objects.

Previously, so that the company was not hindered if it wished to
develop one of its ancillary activities into the main business, the
objects clause generally included a final paragraph making all the
objects into 'main' objects not dependent on each other. It may alter
its objects clause by special resolution. However, under recent
legislation effective from November 1990, if the object is stated as 'to
carry on business as a general commercial company' then the
company may carry on any trade or business whatsoever and has
power to do everything incidental or conducive to that purpose.

The fourth clause of the Memorandum will state that the members
have limited liability and the fifth clause will set out the share
capital.

Ultra vires transactions

At this point it is convenient to mention *ultra vires* transactions. This
is a legal concept but is very important for those managing a
company. *Ultra vires* means 'beyond the power'. Directors, by virtue
of their office and the provisions of the Articles of Association, have
wide responsibility for managing the company, and collectively
have authority to do so. The managing director, as an individual,

not
there
←

fically has authority to bind the company. (The me[n]
[b]und by the Articles, have no right to interfere with the[ir]
[n]s.) The directors must observe any limitation on their po[wer]
[n]g from the Memorandum and Articles, though the compan[y]
[r]atify by Special Resolution any breach of those limitations by
[dir]ectors.

[Howeve]r, since the United Kingdom joined the EEC in 1972 an
ultra [vires tra]nsaction which is entered into by the third party in good
faith, and w[h]ich the directors have decided upon, is enforceable by
the third party against the company. This means that third parties
are given greater protection and can rely on the ostensible authority
of the directors to commit the company, even if those directors are
actually exceeding their powers. In such circumstances the director
concerned may be personally liable to the company, or to the third
party. If the board acts in a way which is beyond its powers the
members in general meeting can ratify the action. Similarly, if one
director exceeds his authority the board can ratify his action.

New legislation has recently been enacted so that, as far as third
parties are concerned the validity of an act done by a company from
November 1990 is not affected by any restriction in the
Memorandum of Association. This means that third parties can rely
on any statement or agreement made by a director to bind the
company.

So in order to function properly without being unduly restricted,
a company needs to have its objects clauses drafted carefully. If a
company is purchased or formed through a company formation
agent, this aspect is usually covered satisfactorily, though it is
always necessary to check the draft objects clause of your new
company, particularly if it is intended to carry on a line of business
which may be slightly unusual or different from the main business.

The Articles of Association
The Articles of Association set out the rules relating to shareholders,
directors, meetings and similar matters of internal administration
under which the company must operate. They relate, among other
things, to:

   share capital, that is the conditions on which it can be allotted, and
      the rights attached to the shares;
   directors, for example conditions regarding appointment and
      retirement;
   secretary, appointment and dismissal;
   meetings of directors and shareholders, for example how often
      they must be held and voting rights;
   some items of administration.

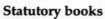

The Company Secretary

...ates that every company must have a set of ... a model set of Articles, referred to as Table ... ot register its own Articles, the appropriate ... apply to it. In practice it is very common to ... lations of Table A while excluding others and ... Articles of the members' choice. The model ... from time to time by legislation, though such ... usually apply to the Articles of existing companies, ... main as they were at the time the company was incorporated unless specially altered.

Statutory books

This is usually one book (bound or loose-leaf) called the Statutory Register with sections on:

members
directors
secretaries
share transfers
applications for, and allotments of shares
directors' interests
debentures
mortgages and charges.

As the name 'register' implies this is a record of matters of importance to the company and it must be kept safely for as long as the company is in existence. The various sections will be dealt with as reference is made to the items which have to be recorded.

Company seal

This is a small hand-operated die press used on certain formal documents which have to be completed by the company. The Articles of Association will include an Article governing the use of the seal.

Other items

Book of Share Certificates. This may be combined with the Statutory Register. A share certificate will have to be prepared each time any shares are issued or transferred. The procedure is described in Chapter 8.

Signed share transfer forms in respect of the shares belonging to the first two subscribers who acted as nominees in the company formation (if the company was bought off the shelf).

Copies of any company forms which have been lodged. These must

Update
Sw books
←

...d away as at least some of the information on them will be
...t for writing up the Statutory Register.

...pany agent will also send letters of resignation from the first
...d secretary and written resolutions appointing the new
...ecretary (if the company was bought off the shelf).

Draft minutes of the first board meeting. These are dealt with fully
in Chapter 5 pages 48–50.

Warranty regarding liabilities. If the company was purchased off the
shelf the company formation agent should provide a warranty that
it has no undisclosed liabilities and has not previously traded, so
that the buyer knows it is a 'clean' company without tax problems or
liabilities.

— Have Andys shares increase
with TP of business
with TP of
shares. be a maxbre on TP of
business

ER 4

Ready to Start

Now that the company has been acquired and all the necessary documents have been received, the first thing to do is to organise the company into the required format as far as directors, secretary, shares and a number of other items are concerned.

Directors

There are certain matters affecting directors which must be spelt out as they are generally applicable. Directors are the people chosen by the shareholders to manage the affairs of the company by acting collectively as a board. This is their prime responsibility.

The chairman is usually the most senior director and may be executive, that is working within the business, or non-executive. The managing director (if one is appointed) is the most senior executive director and has specific authority, by reason of his office, to commit the company.

Categories

'Director' includes any person occupying the position of director, whatever his actual title. In practice, directors can be grouped according to their roles. Executive directors are those responsible for the day-to-day running of the business, either as working proprietors or full-time salaried managers. Non-executive directors are those who have directorial responsibility but do not deal with day-to-day affairs. They might be:

professional non-executive directors, for example an accountant (but not the auditor), to advise on tax and legal issues;
family directors; or
those representing particular shareholders.

It is bad practice to give the title of direc[...] [...]
actually a director of the company, for exa[...]
is in charge of the sales team but not on th[...]
but is not a director. Similar considerat[...]
such as 'marketing director'. Outsiders [...]
thinking that people with such titles a[...]
company could be bound to honour co[...]
even though they have acted outside th[...]

Disqualifications
There are some restrictions on the appointment of directors.

A person may not be both the sole director of a company and its
secretary.
Undischarged bankrupts may not be directors; neither may those
guilty of fraud against the company or who have been
convicted by indictment.
Persons who are disqualified by a Court Order (a fairly rare
occurrence) may not be directors.

Appointment
The first director or group of directors is appointed by the
subscribers to the Memorandum and Articles of Association and is
named on a form sent to the Registrar with the Memorandum and
Articles when applying for registration of the company.

All companies must have at least one director, and often the
Articles specify more. There may be a maximum number. The
directors, as a body, are called the 'board'. A private company need
have only one director, but this person may not also be the
secretary. However, if there are two or more directors, one of them
may hold the office of secretary.

After the first appointments, directors are usually appointed by
the board and provisions governing this are included in the Articles.
Directors appointed in this way have to retire formally and stand for
election at the next annual general meeting if the Articles follow the
Table A example. In many companies the Articles provide that one-
third of the directors must retire by rotation each year. They can, of
course, be re-elected. This is dealt with more fully in Chapter 6 page
57.

The company formation agent will have sent letters of resignation
from the first director and secretary (if the company was bought off
the shelf) with a signed resolution appointing the new director and
secretary (the space for the names may be left blank for you to fill in).
Assuming that only one director has been named in this resolution

nd that you wish to have two directors, whom we shall
ith and Mrs Brown for convenience, the board minutes
rafted to appoint Mrs Brown as a director from a (probably
it) date.

the company was formed at your request the first directors and
ecretary will be those persons you nominated and the foregoing
procedure will not be necessary.

To complete the formalities a Companies Form G288 (see Figure
4.1) will have to be completed with the names, addresses and other
details of the two directors (including dates of birth), signed by each
of them to indicate their acceptance of the appointment, signed by
the secretary (or one of the directors) and despatched to the
Registrar of Companies. This must be done before the expiry of 14
days from the date of appointment. No fee is payable, but care
should be taken to keep a copy of the Form G288 or a note of its
contents, for this will be needed when the Register of Directors is
written up. In the case of an off-the-shelf company it may be
necessary to notify the resignations of the first director(s) on Form
G288 if the company formation agent has not already done so. The
Registrar will not issue a receipt for a company form unless it is sent
with a self-addressed letter or card, on which the identifying details
of the form have been entered, with a request that it be stamped and
returned as an acknowledgement.

Powers, duties and responsibilities

The board of directors has wide powers to manage the company's
affairs and to bind the company legally, particularly since the
European Communities Act and Companies Act 1989 effectively
overrode much of the *ultra vires* doctrine described on page 18. In
law every director of a company (other than the managing director)
has equal powers and responsibilities, whether executive or non-
executive. However, their powers may be limited by the
Memorandum and Articles of Association, (which usually provide
that the directors have authority to manage the company) or by any
restrictions placed on them by the members (usually by means of a
resolution passed at a general meeting).

Directors' duties include managing the affairs of the company to
the best of their ability in the best interests of the company as a
whole, and they are ultimately responsible for everything done by
every one of the company's employees. The Articles of Association
usually set out any limits on the authority of directors, both when
acting collectively as a board and as individuals.

The board acts as a body by passing resolutions, which should be
minuted formally, as set out in Chapter 5, page 40. The board can,

Figure 4.1. *Companies Form G288*

G

COMPANIES FORM No. 288

Notice of change of directors or secretaries or in their particulars

288

Pursuant to section 288 of the Companies Act 1985

Please complete
legibly, preferably
in black type, or
bold block lettering

To the Registrar of Companies

For official use

Company number

Name of company

* insert full name
of company

. SMITH, BROWN AND ROBINSON

ø specify the
change and
date thereof
and if this
consists of the
appointment of
a new director
or secretary
complete the
box below
If this space is
insufficient use
a continuation
sheet

notifies you of the following change(s):

ø MR S. SMITH WAS APPOINTED A DIRECTOR ON --- NOVEMBER ---

Particulars of new director or secretary (see note 1)

Name (note 2 and 3) SMITH, SAMUEL

Business occupation§
CONFECTIONER

Previous name(s) (note 2)

Nationality§
BRITISH

Address (notes 3 and 4) 12 THE AVENUE
NEWTOWN

Postcode

§ Applicable to
directors only.

Date of birth (where applicable)
(note 5)§ 1/4/40

Other directorships (note 6)§ NONE

† delete as
appropriate

I consent to act as [director][secretary] of the company named above

Signature S Smith

Date— NOVEMBER —

Continued overleaf

Presentor's name address and
reference (if any):

For official Use
General Section

Post room

Page 1

Particulars of new director or secretary (see note 1) continued

Name (note 2 and 3)	Business occupation§	§ applicable to directors only.
Previous name(s) (note 2)	Nationality§	
Address (notes 3 and 4)		
Postcode	Date of birth (where applicable) (note 5)§	
Other directorships (note 6)§		
		† delete as appropriate
		‡ insert Director, Secretary, Administrator, Administrative Receiver or Receiver (Scotland) as appropriate
I consent to act as [director] [secretary]† of the company named on page 1		
Signature	Date	

number of continuation sheets attached (see note 7)

Signature **H. Jones**   Designation‡ **SECRETARY**   Date · · **NOVEMBER** --

Notes

1 'Director' includes any person who occupies the position of a director, by whatever name called, and any person in accordance with whose directions or instructions the directors of the company are accustomed to act.

2. For an individual, his present christian name(s) and surname must be given, together with any previous Christian name(s) or surname(s).

"Christian name" includes a forename. In the case of a peer or person usually known by a title different from his surname, "surname" means that title. In the case of a corporation, its corporate name must be given.

A previous christian name or surname need not be given if:—

(a) in the case of a married woman, it was a name by which she was known before her marriage; or

(b) it was changed or ceased to be used at least 20 years ago, or before the person who previously used it reached the age of 18; or

(c) in the case of a peer or a person usually known by a British title different from his surname, it was a name by which he was known before he adopted the title or succeeded to it

3 Where all the partners in a firm are joint secretaries, only the firm's name and its principal office need be given.

Where the secretary or one of the joint secretaries is a Scottish firm, give only the firm name and its principal office.

4 Usual residential address must be given. In the case of a corporation, give the registered or principal office.

5 Date of birth need only be given if the company making the return is:—

(a) a public company;
(b) the subsidiary of a public company; or
(c) the subsidiary of a public company registered in Northern Ireland

6 The names must be given of all bodies corporate incorporated in Great Britain of which the director is also a director, or has been a director at any time during the preceding five years.

However a present or past directorship need not be disclosed if it is, or has been, held in a body corporate which, throughout that directorship, has been:—

(a) a dormant company (which is a company which has had no transactions required to be entered in the company's accounting records, except any which may have arisen from the taking of shares in the company by a subscriber to the memorandum as such).

(b) a body corporate of which the company making the return was a wholly-owned subsidiary;

(c) a wholly-owned subsidiary of the company making the return; or

(d) a wholly-owned subsidiary of a body corporate of which the company making the return was also a wholly owned subsidiary.

7 If the space overleaf is insufficient, the names and particulars must be entered on the prescribed continuation sheet(s).

Page 2

Note. Form 288 will be revised in autumn 1990.

and often does, delegate certain powers and responsibilities to individual directors, who (apart from the managing director) otherwise have no automatic authority when acting on their own.

The Articles usually contain a clause whereby the company indemnifies the directors (and other officers) against losses they may incur in dealing with the company's business, but this does not supersede the normal responsibilities of a director to act properly. A company may take out insurance cover (called Directors and Officers Liability Insurance, or DOLI for short) against liabilities to third parties incurred personally by directors and officers arising from action taken in the course of their duties for the company. Professional advice should be obtained if such insurance is being considered.

Directors have certain specific duties regarding:

the preparation of accounts;
the convening of meetings; and
ensuring that minutes are taken and kept.

They are also subject to certain disclosure requirements to ensure that they do not improperly obtain advantages through their powerful position. Under the Companies Acts a company may make loans to its directors only in a few specific circumstances, and such a loan must not exceed £2500 (which limit will shortly be increased to £5000). There are also restrictions on substantial property deals and other transactions involving directors.

The Registrar of Companies requires a considerable amount of information about each director, by various returns. Any changes in that information must also be recorded and filed within strict time limits. It is also necessary for other records to be kept, for example the number of shares held by directors, and where directors' service contracts are kept.

Directors have a fiduciary responsibility to their company, that is they are bound to act for the company's benefit with high standards of integrity as they are entrusted by the shareholders with the management of the assets owned by the shareholders. They have to carry out their duties of managing the assets and business of the company in the best interests of the shareholders. They must not usurp or abuse their office for personal gain. They also have a statutory duty to have regard to the interests of the company's employees. In addition they have, on behalf of the company, a responsibility to third parties – suppliers, customers, and the public – to fulfil their obligations. Note too their position with regard to insolvency and fraud described on page 30.

Disclosure of interests

Every director must avoid conflicts of interest and must never put himself in a position where his own interests and his obligations as a director may conflict. Directors are required to disclose certain facts about themselves which might influence their dealings with the company, such as their interests in any contract to which the company may be a party, and their shareholdings in the company. The interest in contracts also extends to their interest (directorship or shareholding) in any other company with which the company may make a contract and includes an interest of their spouses and of their children under the age of 18 years.

Every director must formally declare to the company his shareholding in the company (even though the information may already be shown clearly in the Register of Members) and the secretary must ensure that these declarations are entered in the Register of Directors' Interests. Shareholdings in other companies with which the company may have contracts must also be notified to the secretary who should record them in the Register of Directors' Interests after they have been noted at a board meeting. In practice this is generally applied when the shareholding is 5 per cent or more of the equity of the other company.

Directorships of all other companies incorporated in the United Kingdom must be notified to the secretary immediately they arise. The secretary should arrange for them to be noted at a board meeting and entered in the Register of Directors, and notified to the Registrar of Companies on Form G288.

The practice of notifying these interests when they first arise is to avoid the possibility that notification may be overlooked later when a contract is being considered. This would not only be illegal but would give rise to the possibility that the company might claim back from the director any financial advantage which may have been gained unknown to the company. It is also necessary for a director to notify all other directorships that have been held at any time in the five preceding years and these must also be entered in the Register and on Form G288.

A director's interest in a contract being entered into by the company must be declared at a board meeting at the time when the contract in question is under consideration. Such an interest may be direct, that is the director or a member of his or her immediate family is a party to the contract, or indirect, that is when the director or a member of his or her immediate family is connected in some way with the other party to the contract. Usually the Articles provide that a director who is personally interested in a contract is not allowed to vote on the matter when it is being decided upon at a board meeting.

If the contract deals with a transaction relating to prop[...]
be reported in the annual accounts which are sent to share[...]
the end of the year in which it takes place. If the value[...]
transaction is substantial (defined as the lesser of 10 per cent o[...]
company's net assets or £50,000) the *prior* approval of th[...]
shareholders at a general meeting must be obtained before the
contract is completed.

It should be reiterated that the interests of a director include not
only personal interests, but also those of a spouse and children
under 18, as well as any interests through trusts, either as trustee or
as a beneficiary. Directors' interests in the shares of the company
have to be set out in the Directors' Report each year.

Service contracts

Directors may be given service contracts, that is contracts of
employment, setting out their remuneration and conditions of
employment. Even if such contracts are not set out in writing there
will be implied contracts (see the Employment Protection
(Consolidation) Act 1978).

Copies of every director's service contract (or a memorandum
setting out the main terms and conditions if there is no written
contract) if it is not terminable by the company without
compensation within 12 months, must be available for inspection by
any member, that is shareholder. If these copies are not kept at the
registered office the Registrar of Companies must be notified on
Form G318 of the place where they are kept.

The approval of the members in general meeting must be
obtained if it is desired to give a director a contract of service which
cannot be terminated by the company within five years. However,
this situation seldom arises in small private companies and will not
be considered further here.

Fees, salaries and National Insurance

Directors, particularly non-executive directors, are often paid
directors' fees, rather than salaries, in recognition of the services
they render to the company. The amount of the fees may be laid
down in the Articles, or may be decided by the board. Payment of
fees is made under the usual PAYE arrangements unless the
Inspector of Taxes agrees otherwise, and the National Insurance
position is complicated, especially where an individual receives fees
in respect of more than one non-executive directorship. This should
be checked with the Inspector of Taxes.

Executive directors are usually paid a salary and the usual rules
relating to payments of salary apply.

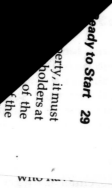

rs to carry on trading as a company
ʋ, that the company is insolvent, th
ions. There are provisions desig
rds of competence and honesty
buses of limited liability. Two penalt

iit' directors; and

ıl liability for company debts on directors
who h... ... olved in a company's 'wrongful' trading.

When a company becomes insolvent the Secretary of State may seek a Court Order disqualifying a director from holding that office in any company for a minimum period of two years. If an insolvent company is wound up and it can be shown that any director knew or ought to have concluded at some previous time that there was no reasonable prospect of the company's avoiding going into insolvent liquidation, that director may be made liable to contribute to the company's assets unless it can be shown that the director took all the steps that should have been taken to prevent that outcome. It is therefore very important that directors should ensure that they know the financial position of the company, and they should not continue to trade if they are aware that the company is unlikely to be able to pay its debts. If trade is bad they should keep in close touch with their accountant and auditor to ensure that they do not break the law in this respect.

Loans

Directors are not allowed to borrow money from their company except to a very limited extent, for example as a float to meet expenses they will have to incur on behalf of the company, and it must be accounted for within six months. Apart from this the maximum amount of any loan is limited to £2500 (which will shortly be increased to £5000). Loans include all kinds of credit, including providing guarantees to third parties of indebtedness, and paying credit card accounts where the goods and services are for the director's personal use. All such loans have to be reported to shareholders in the Directors' Report (which is described in Chapter 7, page 64).

Secretary

Appointment

In addition to one or more directors, every company must have a secretary. Any individual may act as secretary for a private company, the only disqualification being that a sole director cannot also be the secretary. The secretary is an officer of the company and the Articles usually give power to the directors to appoint and remove the secretary.

Notice of the first appointment is sent with the Memorandum and Articles to the Registrar of Companies when the company agent applies for registration.

If the company was bought off the shelf the company formation agent will have nominated one of their staff as the first secretary of the company. When you purchase the company you will find among the documents a letter of resignation from that secretary and the directors will have to appoint a new secretary at the first board meeting (this is included in the draft minutes of the board meeting Figure 5.2, pages 44–45).

The name and other details of the newly appointed secretary will have to be entered on Company Form G288, like those of the new directors – indeed there is space on the printed form for several entries and they can all be done at once – and the form sent to the Registrar of Companies. No fee is payable. This procedure will not be necessary if the company was formed at your request, as your nominee will have been appointed as the first secretary. A copy of the company form should be kept as it will be needed when entering up the Register of Secretaries in due course. It is always good practice to keep either a copy of every company form which is lodged, or at least a very clear record of each one.

In our example of the typical company in Figure 6.3 the secretary is Mrs Jones.

Duties

Generally speaking, the secretary is responsible for ensuring that the company operates within the statutory requirements as detailed in the Companies Acts and described here, and for setting up and maintaining the company's statutory books and records. These duties include ensuring that the company and board act in accordance with the Articles. The secretary has implied authority to enter into contracts connected with the administrative side of the company's affairs, and in many companies is effectively the chief administrative officer of the company, often dealing with insurance, personnel, and property matters, for example, in this capacity.

The secretary is also expected to advise the directors on a variety of legal and administrative matters as well as being responsible for looking after the company seal and important documents which belong to the company; these would include:

gisters
oks

ds of property; these are often held at the bank as security
the secretary should know where they are
ma trading contracts and agreements
insurance policies.

Documents such as leases, title deeds, contracts etc should be listed in a register, assigned an identification number and then filed, preferably in a safe or fireproof filing cabinet. It is usually possible to arrange for the bank to keep them safely, though there may be a charge, and it is helpful in such cases to have a copy in the office for reference purposes. Copies should also be provided to those people in the company who need to refer to the documents for working purposes.

The secretary should also keep a diary of significant dates relating to these documents, such as renewal dates of leases, as a reminder to take action, even if this is not required for several years.

Penalties

The statutes lay a number of duties upon the secretary, and as one of the people (in addition to the directors and the auditor) who is specifically defined as an officer, the secretary is liable to penalties in certain circumstances if he, or the company, neglects or fails to comply with the requirements laid down.

Penalties may be imposed on individual directors and the secretary for breach of statutory requirements, as well as on the company itself. For example, if the annual return is not filed, a fine of up to £2000 may be levied upon the directors and the secretary. It has been held in court that the secretary, by the very nature of the office, is responsible for a number of administrative matters connected with the running of the company, and is therefore liable in law for failure to comply with the statutory requirements.

Subscribers' shares

A typical company will have a nominal capital of £100 divided into 100 shares of a nominal value of £1 each. When the company is formed it is necessary for two shares to be issued. These are the subscribers' shares, which means that the two individuals who have formally signed the application to the Registrar to form the company (two members of the company formation agent's firm for an off-the-shelf company) have indicated that they are each willing to subscribe for one share in the company. These two shares will be the subscribers' shares, and the company formation agent will supply two share transfer forms signed by the subscribers so that these two shares may be transferred into the names of the new owner(s) (see the action list in Figure 4.2). Note that there must always be two shareholders in a company, so these two shares must not be transferred to one person.

At the first board meeting approval must be given for these transfers to be registered. The original subscribers will not usually have paid the subscription money (normally £1 per share) to the company and the new owners will have to do this. Following the meeting the appropriate entries in the statutory books must be made, as set out in Chapter 8, page 73.

If the company was formed to your order, the subscribers' shares will be issued to the people you nominated, so no transfers will be necessary. However, the entries in the statutory books (Register of Members) and payment of the subscription money will still have to be made.

The registered office

The registered office of a company is the formal address of the company which is registered at Companies House and to which formal communications are addressed. Notices under agreements, communications from the Registrar of Companies, writs and summonses will all be addressed to the registered office.

Establishing the registered office

The address of the first registered office will be included in the documents lodged with the Registrar when the company is formed. This will probably have to be changed when the company is bought from the company formation agent (see page 16), unless the company has been formed to order, when the desired address will have been notified to the Registrar.

It is not essential that the registered office be the main, or any other, place of business of the company: it can be the address of the home of the secretary or a director, the office of the company's accountant or lawyer, or any other convenient place. It must, however, be in the country in which the company is incorporated.

The location also determines which Inspector of Taxes will deal with the company's tax affairs, the local Inspector being automatically responsible.

The statutory books of the company must be kept at the registered office unless formal notice has been given to the Registrar on Company Form G318, 325 or 353 (see the list of such forms in Figure

Figure 4.2. *Action list 1: transfer of shares*

TRANSFER OF SHARES

Transferor's name ....

Number of shares ....

Transferee's name ....

Action taken
(Date)

1. Obtain Share Transfer Form (STF) ....

2. Obtain old share certificate ....

3. Check STF (a) signature
        (b) transferor particulars agree
            with Register of Members
        (c) share certificate equals or
            exceeds number of shares
            transferred
        (d) STF is properly stamped ....

4. Obtain board approval for registration ....

5. Enter Register of Transfers ....

6. Enter Register of Members (a) transferor
            (b) transferee ....

7. Prepare new share certificate and cancel
    old certificate ....

8. Prepare balance certificate if necessary ....

9. Have share certificates sealed and signed ....

10. Enter in Register of Directors' Interests
    (if a director is involved) ....

6.1 page 56) that they are kept at another place. Each form refers to a particular Register; the Register of Directors must be kept at the registered office and nowhere else.

The registered office may be moved to another address if desired. If this is done a formal notice must be given to the Registrar on form G287 within 14 days of the change. There will be two main consequences of the change. First, the information on the company's headed paper and other printed stationery will have to be changed, and second (unless the new address is within the same tax district) a new Inspector of Taxes will become responsible for the company's tax affairs, which may cause difficulties until the new Inspector becomes as familiar with them as the previous one. An action list setting out the steps involved in changing the situation of the registered office is given in Figure 4.3.

The full name of the company must be displayed on the outside of every office or place of business and in all notices and publications of the company; including cheques, orders, invoices, statements etc. This includes advertisements inviting the public to order goods by post.

Figure 4.3. *Action list 2: change of registered office*

CHANGE OF REGISTERED OFFICE

New registered office address . . . .

. . . .

Date of change . . . .

Action taken
(Date)

1. Board resolution   . . . .

2. Notify Registrar of Companies (Form G287) . . . .

3. Arrange for name plate(s) to be displayed   . . . .

4. Amend headed paper etc   . . . .

5. Check if statutory books are to be kept at
    new registered office address. If not,
    notify Registrar of Companies on Form
    G318, 325, or 353   . . . .

Stationery

The company's headed paper must show the full name of the company, its registered number, the place of registration (expressed either as England and Wales, Wales, or Scotland as appropriate) and the address of the registered office. This address will either be in addition to the address of the place of business if the latter is different, or if it is the same that fact must be clearly stated. An example of a notepaper heading is shown below. The names of the directors may be shown on the headed paper through it is not necessary to do so. However, it is not permissible to show the names of some, but not all, of them except in special circumstances. The nationality of a director must be shown against his name if he is not a national of a European Community country.

The requirement to show this information on headed paper extends also to order forms, which means forms provided by the company on which prospective customers can order goods from the company.

Figure 4.4 *Sample of headed paper*

SMITH, BROWN AND ROBINSON LIMITED

5 West Street,
Newtown NE8 1AW
England.
Telephone 00000 000
Fax 00000 000

VAT Registration No 0000000 00
Company No 123456   Registered in England and Wales
Registered Office: 1 High Street, Newtown, England.

---

e of a business name

ay be that the business is carried on under a trading name which
»t the proper name of the company; for example, Smith, Brown
and Robinson Limited may trade as Smith's Newsagents. In such a
case stationery may have the trading name (usually referred to as a
business name) shown prominently, but in addition the full name of
the company must also appear and it must also be shown clearly
outside the business premises.

Company seal

When the seal is received it should be formally adopted by the board
as the common seal of the company. A minute should be passed,
like the example shown in Figure 5.2, pages 44–45, and the seal
impressed at the foot of the page in the Minute Book. The same
procedure should be followed if the seal has to be changed, for
example following a change of name of the company.

It is no longer essential to have a company seal, and a formal
document will be properly executed if it is signed by two directors,
or a director and the secretary, and contains words to the effect that
it is intended to be a deed.

Accounting reference date

All companies are allowed to select, within nine months of the date
of their incorporation, the accounting reference date (ARD) of their
choice, that is the date on which their financial year (accounting
reference period or ARP) is to end. If the company fails to make a
decision, which has to be notified to the Registrar of Companies on
Form G224 (see page 52), the ARD is automatically the last day of the
month in which the anniversary of its incorporation falls. For
companies incorporated before 1 April 1990 the ARD was
automatically 31 March if no alternative date had been notified.

If, later, it is desired to change the accounting reference date the
board must pass a formal resolution and the new date has to be
notified to the Registrar on Form G225(1). A draft of a suitable
minute is given overleaf. However, there are limitations on what
changes can be made. If the decision is made during the course of
the ARP, then the ARD can be brought forward, that is earlier, as
much as is desired. It can only be put back for the maximum of six
months, that is the ARP can only be extended to 18 months at most.
If the existing ARD has already passed no retrospective alteration
can be made except on takeover or amalgamation of companies (and
this situation is not dealt with here).

Figure 4.5.   *A suitable minute changing the accounting reference date*

IT WAS RESOLVED that the accounting reference date of the
Company be changed to XX XXXXXXXXX 19XX, effective in
respect of the accounting reference period which commenced
on XX XXXXXXXXX 19XX.

It should be noted that a company is not permitted to extend its ARP
more frequently than once in every five years, except in very special
circumstances, so that any proposed change must be carefully
considered as it may not be possible to make another change quickly
in normal circumstances.

The company's accountant or auditor will be able to advise on
whether a change of ARD is permissible.

Auditor

All companies must have an auditor who is regarded as the
shareholders' watchdog. His role is to check that the financial affairs
of the company as summarised in the annual accounts have been
carried on in a proper fashion and that the accounts accurately
record the various transactions which have taken place. The auditor
is a professional accountant who will probably also prepare the final
annual accounts and audit them. For most practical purposes small
companies have one accountant, possibly part time, who provides
the necessary accounting services. The auditor and accountant may
be one person but in the legal sense they are different personalities,
and therefore may be referred to as 'the auditor' (for legal purposes)
or 'the accountant' (when dealing with accounting matters
generally).

It is possible to dispense with the annual appointment of auditors
by passing an elective resolution (see page 57), and the auditors are
then deemed to be re-appointed automatically. If it is desired to take
advantage of this facility the subject should be discussed first with
the auditor, as it might be that it would also be desirable to dispense
with holding AGMs and laying accounts before members thereat.
The whole subject should be considered at one time.

The appointment of the first auditor will be made by the directors,
and will be confirmed by the members at the first annual general
meeting. Subsequently the auditor will be reappointed by the
members at each annual general meeting at which accounts are laid
before the members. This emphasises that the auditor is acting on

behalf of the shareholders, though of course he may well advise the directors on many matters of a financial nature relating to the activities of the company.

It is desirable to meet a partner of the firm of auditors who are being considered for appointment before the matter is settled. If you do not know of any suitable firms, the Institute of Chartered Accountants in England and Wales or, in Scotland, the Institute of Chartered Accountants of Scotland, will provide a list of names and addresses.

The procedure for changing auditors is precisely defined by legislation and is set out in Chapter 8, page 92.

Opening a bank account

The company will need a bank account and the directors should decide which bank and which branch will provide the services required. It should be remembered that, apart from normal current account facilities, overdraft or loan facilities may be required, and it is wise to discuss the matter with the bank manager before making a decision.

Once a bank has been chosen, the manager will provide a standard form of board resolution needed by the bank to open the account. This form will have to be approved by the board as a resolution and a copy, signed by the chairman of the meeting and the secretary, is then sent to the bank, with specimen signatures of those persons authorised to sign cheques on behalf of the company. Sometimes two signatures are needed but this may cause administrative delay, particularly if only one of the individuals works in the business; on the other hand, it may provide a safeguard against error or fraud. A useful compromise is to require only one signature for cheques for small sums, say £100 or less, and two signatures for larger amounts.

CHAPTER 5

Running the Company

This chapter describes some of the general rules relating to board meetings and the preparation of minutes of those meetings – a job which falls naturally to the secretary. The initial entries in the statutory books, and the statutory forms which have to be lodged with the Registrar, are also described.

Board meetings

In order to run a business the managers, ie the directors of a company, usually have to consult each other, perhaps frequently. Some of these meetings have to be on a formal basis so that the decisions taken are recorded as board minutes, which form a statutory record. Decisions taken at board meetings often give rise to formal company secretarial work, and examples are described below.

Holding a meeting

Formal meetings of the board must be held when certain items require decision. It may also be useful for the directors to meet at intervals to discuss the affairs of the company as a whole, particularly if any of the directors are non-executive, that is not involved in the day-to-day business of the company. The Articles will require that minutes be kept of the decisions taken. Apart from these meetings the directors have authority to take decisions relating to the business of the company; refer to the paragraph on ostensible authority and *ultra vires* transactions in Chapter 3, pages 18–19.

The Articles may make special provision for board meetings; otherwise they will be held as necessary. As a minimum one board meeting should be held each year, when the directors have to approve the Directors' Report and the accounts, authorise the convening of the annual general meeting and deal with any other formal matters which have accumulated.

As an alternative to holding a board meeting it is possible (if the Articles permit) to make a decision by circulating a written resolution for signature by *all* directors (see page 47).

The first board meeting
Once the company has been formed or acquired it will be necessary to hold a board meeting to deal with a number of formal items. The agenda (which should indicate clearly the time, date and place of the meeting) should be issued beforehand (see Figure 5.1).

The company formation agent will probably have provided some formal resolutions arising from the incorporation of the company and these should be noted; they may cover some of the other items listed below.

Notice of a meeting
Reasonable notice of a meeting must be given to all directors except those outside the UK, unless the company's Articles state otherwise. Seven days' notice is reasonable unless it is easy to contact all directors at shorter notice and there is no problem about their attendance. Unless all directors have been given reasonable notice, the meeting is not properly constituted and no valid decisions can be made. Failure to give proper notice invalidates the meeting and any decisions taken at it unless *all* directors agree to waive the notice requirement. Their agreement should be minuted and the agreement of any absent director obtained in writing.

Agenda
The agenda for the first board meeting of an off-the-shelf company will usually include the following items (see also Figure 5.1).

*These items will not be necessary if the company was formed to your order, though it is sensible to note any appointments of directors and secretary which have been made.

noting the Certificate of Incorporation
approval of:
    transfers of shares from subscribers*
    appointment of the directors of your choice*
    appointment of the secretary*
    adoption of the common seal
noting resolutions of the previous directors if the company is
    newly acquired from a company agent*
location of Registered Office*

appointment of auditors
appointment of bankers
deciding on the accounting reference date
allotment of shares and issue of share certificates.

If the company has been formed to take over an existing business
it will have to buy that business from the present owner (who may
well not be the person who has arranged the formation of the
company). It is usually necessary for a formal contract to be drawn
up (preferably by a solicitor) whereby the vendor and the company
agree to transfer the ownership of the business on a certain date at
an agreed price. The price may be satisfied by:

the issue of shares in the company (see Chapter 8 page 86) which
    is quite usual if the vendor is also the owner, that is to say the
    shareholder, of the company; or
cash, which would necessitate the company's borrowing money
    or issuing shares to third parties for cash; or
a mixture of cash and shares.

Board decisions will be needed to deal with these matters.
There may be other matters to discuss as well, such as:

the leasing or purchase of premises;
loans and/or bank overdrafts.

In practice these matters will usually have been considered before
the meeting, and are put to the board for formal approval.

At the meeting the secretary should see that all necessary
decisions are taken and will take notes in order to prepare the
minutes later. All necessary papers for reference or signature should
be available and the secretary should generally help to expedite the
business. After the meeting the secretary will prepare the minutes
and, depending on the organisation of the company, may be
responsible for implementing or arranging the implementation of
the board's decisions. A draft set of minutes of the first board meeting
for an off-the-shelf company is shown in Figure 5.2 on page 44.

Quorum

A quorum is the minimum number of people who must be present
to transact business validly. A board meeting cannot legally be held
with only one person present, unless there is only one director on
the board. If the company has only one director board meetings can
be held by that director. The quorum for a meeting is normally a
minimum of two people (how can it be a meeting if only one person
is present?) but may be more than this for a board meeting or a
general meeting if the Articles provide for a larger figure.

Figure 5.1. *Agenda for first board meeting*

SMITH, BROWN AND ROBINSON LIMITED

Agenda for Board Meeting to be held on 1 November 19XX at
1 High Street, Newtown at 10.00 am

A G E N D A

1. To note and approve as necessary
   (a) Certificate of Incorporation;
   (b) transfers of shares;
   (c) appointment of director;
   (d) appointment of secretary;
   (e) previous directors' resolution (if any);
   (f) adoption of Common Seal.

2. To appoint auditors.

3. To appoint bankers.

4. To fix Accounting Reference Date.

5. To appoint additional director.

6. To allot shares.

7. Any other business.

8. Date of next meeting.

It is not a legal requirement to appoint a chairman, but it usually helps the conduct of business to do so and, in practice, the senior director is often appointed chairman by vote of the board.

Voting
Voting is rarely necessary at board meetings. The chairman's role is to sense the feeling of the meeting and spell out the decisions. If it is necessary to vote formally at a board meeting the chairman puts the motion to the vote. In the event of an equality of votes for and

against the motion, the chairman has a second, casting vote if the Articles permit a casting vote.

The names of those voting for and against are not usually recorded. However, if any directors particularly wish to record their disagreement with the decision taken, they may request a note of this fact to be included in the minutes.

Figure 5.2. *Draft minutes of first board meeting*

SMITH, BROWN AND ROBINSON LIMITED

Minutes of Board Meeting held on 1 November 19XX at High Street, Newtown

Present: Mr S Smith
Mrs B Brown

In Attendance: Mrs H Jones (Secretary)

1. There were produced to the Meeting:

    (a) the Certificate of Incorporation dated 17 October 19XX

    (b) the two transfers of the subscribers' shares as follows:

TRANSFEROR	SHARES	TRANSFEREE
Mrs T Taylor	1 Ordinary share	Mr S Smith
Mr R Morrison	1 Ordinary share	Mrs B Brown

    (c) the notice of appointment of the director (Mr Smith)

    (d) the notice of appointment of a new secretary (Mrs Jones)

    (e) resignation of the first director (Mrs T Taylor)

    (f) resignation of the first secretary (Mr J Jackson)

    (g) notice of situation of registered office.

    IT WAS RESOLVED

    (a) to note the above documents;

    (b) to approve:

        (i) adoption of the common seal of which an impression is made hereon as the common seal of the company;

Figure 5.2. *Draft minutes of first board meeting (continued)*

   (ii) subject to their agreement, appointment of Black, Jacques & Co as auditors of the company at a fee to be agreed;

  (iii) appointment of Money Bank Ltd as bankers to the company and resolutions were passed in accordance with the bank forms produced to the meeting;

  (iv) the transfers of the subscribers' shares and, after stamping by the Inland Revenue, their registration.

2. ACCOUNTING REFERENCE DATE

IT WAS RESOLVED that the company's accounting reference date be 31st March.

3. DIRECTORATE

IT WAS RESOLVED to appoint Mrs B Brown a director of the company with immediate effect.

4. ALLOTMENT OF SHARES

Forms of application as listed below applying for 98 shares of £1 each were produced and the receipt of £98, being payment in full therefore, was reported. It was also reported that £2 had been received in payment in full for the subscribers' shares.

IT WAS RESOLVED

(a) that 98 shares of £1 each, fully paid and numbered from 3 to 100 inclusive, be and are hereby allotted to the following persons:

Applicant/Allottee	No of Shares
Mr S Smith	39
Mrs B Brown	39
Mrs T Smith	10
Mr C Brown	10

(b) that the shares of the company shall henceforth cease to bear distinguishing numbers.

(c) that the sealing and issue of share certificates for 100 shares of £1 each, fully paid, drawn in respect of the subscribers' shares and the said allotment, be authorised.

(d) that the secretary be instructed to file the statutory return of allotments.

Note: If a new Secretary is to be appointed the Minute should follow Number 3 above with the word 'Director' changed to 'Secretary'. Minute 1(d) may need alteration or omission.

Procedure for meetings

It is the responsibility of the secretary to organise board meetings.

Before the meeting

the secretary must give notice of the meeting to:
all directors, and
any others who will be required to attend, for example the
company accountant or solicitor.

The notice must include:

time
date
place, and
matters to be considered (the agenda).

The secretary should prepare the agenda and distribute copies in advance. Indeed, this is often incorporated as part of the notice of meeting.

If the purpose of the meeting is to pass formal or detailed resolutions the secretary can circulate these before the meeting in the form of drafts attached to the agenda.

The secretary is also responsible for administrative arrangements:

preparing the directors' attendance book if one is kept;
ensuring that all relevant documents are to hand (including the
minute book); and
booking and preparing the meeting room (and perhaps
refreshments).

At the meeting

If an attendance book is kept (and this may be a requirement in the Articles, though it is less common nowadays) the secretary must see that the directors sign it on arrival. The secretary must then check that the meeting has a quorum according to the Articles, and that it will not be affected by the presence of any director who might not be allowed to vote on an item of business in which he has a personal interest. For example, the company might be leasing or buying a property owned by one of its directors, and that director would not be permitted to vote on the matter because of the possibility of conflict between personal interest and interest as a director of the company. The Articles should be consulted to ascertain the exact position.

When the meeting begins the secretary must report and record apologies for absence.

During the meeting the secretary:

takes notes of proceedings, decisions taken, and instructions
given;

records late arrivals and early departures;

must be ready to advise on the legality of any proposed action and
its position with regard to the Memorandum and Articles;

calls any invited person into the meeting.

After the meeting

After the meeting the secretary must remove all confidential
documents and organise clearance of the room.

If the chairman has made notes of the meeting these should be
passed to the secretary to compare with the secretary's own notes.
Both should be destroyed when the minutes are produced and
signed, so that the minutes remain the only, and authentic, record of
the meeting.

The secretary then prepares draft minutes of the meeting as soon as
possible, for comment by directors and for the information of any
absent directors. When any alterations to the draft have been agreed
and made the minutes are entered in the minute book for signing at
the next meeting. If a director does not agree with a decision this
disagreement should be noted in the minutes.

The minutes can then be presented at the next meeting for
discussion only as to their accuracy as a record before they are signed.
The minutes of a board meeting must be a record of the decisions
taken at that meeting and any discussion which changes decisions in
any way should be recorded in the minutes of the subsequent
meeting.

The secretary may have to notify any managers or other personnel
of any decisions which affect them, take action as instructed at the
meeting, and note any items deferred to a future meeting.

Circulated resolutions

Most Articles state that if a written resolution is circulated and signed
by *all* directors it is a valid alternative to presentation and approval at
a board meeting. The secretary may draft a resolution if it is difficult
for all the directors to attend a meeting at short notice or if the matter
requires a board resolution but does not warrant the calling of a
special meeting. It is not sufficient (unless there is specific provision
in the Articles) for such a resolution to be signed by only so many
directors as would form a quorum for a board meeting. If there are
many directors, or they are widely scattered, it is permissible to
circulate several copies of the resolution and collect all the signatures
by having some on each copy.

This procedure may also be used to approve resolutions for which a General Meeting would otherwise be necessary (other than resolutions for removing a director or the auditor). The document or documents must be signed by *all* members who would be entitled to attend and vote at a general meeting, which means in practice that only companies with a small number of shareholders are likely to be able to take advantage of this facility.

The signed copy (or copies) must then be placed in the minute book in chronological order. The resolution must be dated on the day on which the last signature is obtained and is effective from that date.

Minutes

Minutes must be kept of board, general and directors' committee meetings, and entered in books kept specifically for that purpose. These minute books must be kept throughout the life of the company, however long that may be.

Minutes of general meetings must be kept at the registered office and are available for inspection by any member, but members are not entitled to inspect the minutes of board or directors' committee meetings.

Minutes should not be overloaded with administrative detail. However, they should record decisions which are not automatically part of the regular activities of the company, with a summary of the essential points leading to decisions if necessary. The minutes should also record other decisions relating to matters which may have financial or other consequences which would have a significant effect on the company's business, or which require specific formal authority.

Generally speaking, the minutes record only the decisions taken at a meeting, perhaps preceded by a short narration dealing with the essential points leading to the decision. If the secretary is in doubt as to the decision at the end of a discussion it is best to ask the chairman to be specific so that there can be no dispute later. The secretary should not turn the minutes into a report by setting out the discussion in detail or by referring to individual opinions. These are included only if a director requests a record of any disagreement with a decision taken. A specimen set of board minutes is shown in Figure 5.2.

Writing minutes
Minute taking and writing does require some specialist skills, particularly how to reduce long discussions to concise, instructive minutes. Minutes must be:

accurate
succinct
unambiguous
grammatically correct
useful (nothing inessential)
capable of being understood by other readers.

There are several grammatical rules to be remembered; ignorance of these often causes a breakdown in at least one of the areas already mentioned. Statements by individuals should be recorded as indirect rather than direct speech. Always use accurate terms, recording facts as opposed to generalised statements, for example say 'the company' rather than 'we'. Use the imperfect tense to record events which took place at the meeting and the perfect tense for events which occurred prior to the meeting. Remember that the minutes should be intelligible when read months or years later. If memoranda, reports or other documents are referred to in the minutes they should, if they are not summarised, be attached as appendices if of great importance, or kept safely by the secretary for subsequent reference.

Numbering of minutes
The pages, or individual minutes in a bound book containing the minutes, must be numbered sequentially. The signatures of all the directors, and the date, must be on any resolution passed under the circulated resolution procedure. These resolutions should be inserted in the minute book in chronological order and not as an appendix to the minutes of the next meeting.

Loose-leaf format
Minutes always used to be written or stuck into a firmly bound book, and this procedure may still be followed. However, it is now very common for minutes to be written or typed on loose sheets of paper which are kept in a loose-leaf binder. This practice is permitted subject to proper safeguards to prevent unauthorised alteration or falsification. The binder should preferably have a locking device, with the key kept by the secretary, and should be kept in a safe cabinet.

There are advantages in using loose leaves. They can be put in a typewriter, and when typed several copies can be made for those to whom the minutes are to be sent. Do remember, however, the security aspect of spare copies and masters; minutes often include confidential and valuable information which should not be allowed to reach unauthorised persons.

The sheets of paper should be serially numbered as used, and the chairman, when signing the last page of the minutes, should also initial all other pages. This is for authentication and does not signify that the minutes are approved by the person who signs them. Any alteration to the minute book pages must be initialled by the chairman, though if the minutes are prepared in draft first and then retyped when all comments have been made, there should seldom if ever be occasion to alter the final minutes. A misspelt word or clerical error can be altered and initialled by the chairman when signing the minutes.

The main disadvantage of the loose-leaf format is the risk of unauthorised alteration by substitution of an amended page. The initialling by the chairman is intended to prevent this.

Signature of minutes

It is common practice to include as the first item on the agenda for a meeting an item for approving the signature of the minutes of the previous meeting. This approval is only to the effect that those minutes are a true and correct record of the proceedings at the previous meeting, not that the decisions are being confirmed; if events subsequent to the earlier meeting require a decision to be changed then a fresh minute must be passed, and it is not right to alter the previous minutes to reflect events which happened after the meeting concerned. If the minutes have been previously circulated and the meeting agrees their accuracy the chairman will sign (and date at the date of signature) the last page and initial the other pages. If the minutes were not previously circulated the secretary will read them out before they are signed.

If long intervals elapse between meetings, for example annual general meetings, the minutes can be signed at the next convenient board meeting or, if there is urgency to have signed minutes, by the person who was in the chair at the meeting concerned.

It is lawful for alternative methods of signing and dating minute books to be adopted so long as the secretary is, at all times, satisfied that the security of the minutes is adequately safeguarded.

As soon as the minutes have been signed they can be produced in court as prima facie evidence of the proceedings at the meeting. This is one reason why minutes must not be altered after they have been signed, either by the secretary acting under the instructions of a director or on the secretary's own initiative. No item from an earlier meeting may be altered or deleted but a subsequent minute may be recorded which corrects or alters it.

The omission of an important point may be sufficient for a member to prove at law the inaccuracy of the minutes and have the resolutions of the meeting set aside!

ıinute book must always be kept in a safe place and must
e destroyed while the company is in existence.

ng up the statutory books and statutory returns

: the board meeting the secretary will have to deal with a
number of items, as follows:

Share transfers
The details of the share transfers must be entered in the Register of
Transfers, and in the Register of Members, as set out in Chapter 8,
page 73. It may be that the company formation agent will not have
made the necessary entries to record the subscribers' shares, and if
this is so, these entries should be máde before the transfers are
registered.

Appointment of directors
Details of the new directors must be entered in the Register of
Directors, and if the company formation agent has not entered the
details of the first director, this should be done, taking the
information from the copy of the Company Form G288 (or Form 10
if the company was formed to order) supplied by the agent. A
Company Form G288 must then be made out in respect of any newly
appointed directors, signed by each new director indicating that he
is willing to accept the appointment, and the secretary, and sent
within 14 days to the Registrar of Companies. It is now necessary to
enter the dates of birth of all directors. An action list for this is given
in Figure 5.3 on page 52.

If a director has resigned the Registrar must also be notified on
Company Form 288.

Appointment of secretary
Details of the new secretáry must be entered in the Register of
Secretaries and a Form G288 completed within 14 days, exactly as for
a new director. There is room on the form for several entries, and it
is quite in order to notify changes in directors and secretary on the
same form. Remember to state, in the narrative space at the start of
the form, which directors and secretary are resigning and which are
being appointed. The notes on the back of the form, and the
reference in the *Notes for Guidance of Registered Companies*, give all the
information needed to enable the form to be completed correctly.
An example of a completed Form G288 is given in Figure 4.1 on page
26 and an action list is given in Figure 5.4.

Figure 5.3. *Action list 3: appointment of a director*

DIRECTOR'S APPOINTMENT

NAME ....

DATE OF APPOINTMENT ....

Action taken
(Date)

1. Board resolution ....

2. Issue Company Form G288 ....

3. Issue copy of Memorandum and Articles ....

4. Notify Registrar of Companies ....
   (within 14 days)

5. Notify bankers
   (check authorised signatories) ....

6. Enter up Register of Directors ....

7. Enter up Register of Directors' Holdings ....

8. If share qualification, put transfer action
   in hand ....

9. Add name to stationery
   (if other directors listed) ....

10. Prepare service contract ....

Location of registered office
A Company Form G287 must be sent within 14 days to the Registrar of Companies notifying any change of registered office (see Chapter 4, page 33 and the action list in Figure 4.3 on page 35.

Accounting reference date
When this has been chosen Company Form G224 must be sent to the

Figure 5.4. *Action list 4: appointment/resignation of secretary*

```
┌─────────────────────────────────────────────────────┐
│  SECRETARY'S APPOINTMENT/RESIGNATION                  │
│  ─────────────────────────────────────────────       │
│                                                       │
│  NAME  . . . . . . . . . . . . . . . . . . . . . . .  │
│                                                       │
│  DATE OF APPOINTMENT/RESIGNATION  . . . . . . . . .    │
│                                                       │
│                                         Action taken  │
│                                            (Date)     │
│                                                       │
│  1. Board resolution                    . . . . . . . │
│                                                       │
│  2. Issue Company Form G288                           │
│        (if appointment)                 . . . . . . . │
│                                                       │
│  3. Notify Registrar of Companies                     │
│        (within 14 days)                 . . . . . . . │
│                                                       │
│  4. Notify bankers                                    │
│        (if authorised signatory)        . . . . . . . │
│                                                       │
└─────────────────────────────────────────────────────┘
```

Registrar (see Chapter 4, page 37). Remember that if this is not done within nine months of incorporation, it is automatically the anniversary of the last day of the month in which the company was incorporated.

Allotment of shares
The details of any new shares which are being allotted must be entered in the Register of Allotments and also in the shareholder accounts in the Register of Members for the existing or new shareholders, as appropriate. A Return of Allotments on Form PUC2 must be completed and sent to the Registrar of Companies with a cheque for the capital duty at the rate of £1 for each £100 (or part of £100) of new capital. This return must be sent within one month of the date of allotment.

Appointment of auditors and bankers
The secretary should communicate with the auditors and bankers regarding their appointment.

CHAPTER 6

The Continuing Routines

Once all the necessary action has been completed to get the company started the secretary will probably have many other duties to carry out, and will not be occupied full time on company secretarial matters. However, various events may occur which will require some formal action and some of these will now be described.

Statutory books and returns

The secretary's duties include keeping the statutory books of the company and this involves not only their custody but also writing them up as changes occur which need recording. The various books are listed in Chapter 3, page 20. Consequently, whenever there is a change of director or secretary, or in the particulars (name, address or other directorships held) of any of the individuals, the information must be recorded, and a Company Form G288 will have to be completed and sent to the Registrar.

Equally, any change in the members of the company, whether it be a transfer of their shares, or an alteration in their particulars such as a change of address, must be entered in the Register of Members and, if appropriate, in the Register of Transfers. Changes to these two books do not, however, need to be notified to the Registrar, except as part of the Annual Return. Similar considerations apply to changes in debenture or preference shareholders.

Holders of debentures and preference shares are in some ways like shareholders. Debentures are loans, often arranged under a trust deed which gives certain rights and protection to the lenders, which can be bought and sold by the lenders like ordinary shares. Preference shares are shares (which means that the holders are members of the company) which carry some preferential rights over the ordinary shares. These rights are usually priority over the ordinary shareholders to receive a fixed level of dividend and to receive assets if the company is wound up. The registers of holders of these securities are maintained in exactly the same way as the Register of Members.

The Register of Charges must be kept up to date as explained in Chapter 8, page 81.

Statutory returns must also be sent to the Registrar if any of the following events occur:

change of registered office;
change of accounting reference date;
increase of capital;
allotments of shares;
move of Registers of Members, Debenture Holders, Directors' Interests or copies of directors' service contracts to another place;
particulars of certain mortgages and charges.

A list of commonly used statutory return forms is given in Figure 6.1 and the *Notes for Guidance of Registered Companies*, issued by the Registrar of Companies, refer to these as well as to others.

Board meetings

These have been described generally in Chapter 5. The secretary should bear in mind that the board should approve decisions on matters of significance particularly as the auditors may well wish to check on these, and it is very desirable to record clearly such decisions for later reference. These include:

signing minutes of previous meeting;
opening a bank account and authorising signatories;
arranging an overdraft or bank loan;
taking on property by lease or purchase;
acquiring another business;
appointment of directors or secretary;
remuneration of directors;
noting directors' declarations of interest;
issue and allotment of shares;
transfers of shares;
affixing the common seal to a document;
declaring an interim dividend;
large or unusual items of expenditure.

The arrangements for a board meeting should follow those described in Chapter 5 for the first board meeting.

Figure 6.1. *Commonly used statutory return forms for limited companies*

The following company forms are those used most frequently and mentioned elsewhere in this guide. Copies may be obtained on request from the Registrar of Companies, or purchased from legal stationers.

G123	Notice of Increase in Nominal Capital
G224	Notice of Accounting Reference Date
G225(1)	Notice of new Accounting Reference Date given during the course of an Accounting Reference Period
G225(2)	Notice of new Accounting Reference Date given after the end of an Accounting Reference Period
G287	Notice of Change in Situation of Registered Office
G288	Notice of Change of Directors or Secretaries or in their particulars
G318	Notice of Place where copies of Directors' Service Contracts or any memoranda are kept or of any change in that place
G325	Notice of Place where Register of Directors' Interests in shares is kept or of any change in that place
G353	Notice of Place where Register of Members is kept or of any change in that place
A363	Annual Return of a Company
A386	Notice of passing of Resolution removing an Auditor
M395	Particulars of a Mortgage or Charge
M403a	Declaration of satisfaction in full or in part of mortgage or charge.

Incidentally, the numbers of the forms indicate the numbers of the clauses in the Companies Act 1985 which contain the requirement to notify the information concerned.

PUC 2	Notice of Allotment of Shares.

General meetings

General meetings are meetings of the members of a company to transact certain items of business which are specified in the statutes. These meetings are either Annual General Meetings (AGMs) or Extraordinary General Meetings (EGMs).

The differences between AGMs and EGMs

AGMs are held once a year to deal with a defined series of items, as set out in Figure 6.3 on page 59. Any other general meeting called in the year has to be an EGM, although the procedure for giving notice and conduct of business is essentially the same. An EGM may be convened to deal with an item of business which requires the approval of shareholders, such as change of the name or Articles of the company. If an AGM is due to be held it is possible to deal with such matters as special business at the meeting, but often the timing of the AGM is not fortuitous and an EGM is required.

Special business may be dealt with as ordinary resolutions, or as special or elective resolutions. The Companies Acts specify the category into which various kinds of resolution fall, and a list of typical ones is set out in Figure 6.2. The provisions for giving notice and voting vary slightly according to which kind of resolution is to be passed (see the section dealing with such resolutions on page 58).

Figure 6.2. *List of ordinary, special and elective resolutions*

RESOLUTIONS AT GENERAL MEETINGS

Ordinary Resolutions
Adoption of Directors' Report and accounts (note that these are 'adopted', not 'approved')
Election of directors
Declaration of dividend
Appointment and remuneration of auditors
Authority to directors to allot shares
Increasing authorised capital
Approval of profit sharing share schemes or share option schemes for employees.

Special Resolutions
Changing the name of the Company
Altering the Memorandum of Association
Altering the Articles of Association
Authorising directors to issue shares for cash other than to existing shareholders in proportion to existing shareholdings.

Elective Resolutions
Authority for indefinite period to allot shares
Dispensing with requirement to lay accounts before the AGM
Dispensing with requirement to hold AGM
Dispensing with the annual appointment of auditors

Annual General Meetings

An AGM must be held within 18 months of incorporation and then once each calendar year with an interval of not more than 15 months between one meeting and the next. The meeting is usually convened when the Directors' Report and annual accounts (explained in Chapter 7) are circulated to shareholders. The usual business of an AGM (as set out in the specimen Notice of Meeting (Figure 6.3)) is dealt with by ordinary resolutions.

It is possible to dispense with the requirement to hold Annual General Meetings, by passing an elective resolution. If it is desired to follow this procedure professional advice should be sought on the wording of the resolution.

If such a resolution is passed and AGMs are no longer held, any member may give notice to the company not less than three months before the end of the year requiring the holding of an AGM in that year. The board must then arrange to hold an AGM.

Extraordinary General Meetings

An EGM has to be convened when there is special business to be dealt with by the members if this cannot be covered at an AGM. This will occur when the AGM for the year has already been held (as only one AGM can be held in a year) or is not due to be held within the time available for dealing with the special business concerned.

Examples of business which could require such a meeting to be called are:

changing the name of the company;
altering the Memorandum and/or Articles of Association;
increasing the authorised capital and authorising the directors to allot shares.

Directors are bound to convene an EGM on application by members holding one-tenth or more of the paid-up voting capital of the company.

Resolutions – Ordinary, Special and Elective

Business at general meetings is decided by the passing of resolutions. These are divided into Ordinary Resolutions, Special Resolutions and Elective Resolutions, depending on the subject matter (see also Figure 6.2 on page 57).

Ordinary resolutions include all resolutions other than those classed as special and elective resolutions. The most common example (other than the routine resolutions of AGMs) is a resolution increasing the nominal or authorised capital. Only 14 days' notice is needed to convene a general meeting (other than an AGM, for which

Figure 6.3. *Notice of AGM*

SMITH, BROWN AND ROBINSON LIMITED

Directors:

Mr S Smith
Mrs B Brown

Registered Office

1 High Street
Newtown NE8 1AX
England.
Telephone: 0686 0001

8th June 19XX

NOTICE OF ANNUAL GENERAL MEETING

Notice is hereby given that the Annual General Meeting of the Company will be held at the registered office of the Company on 30th June 19XX at 12 o'clock for the following purposes:

1. To receive and adopt the Directors' Report and the Accounts for the year ended 31st March 19XX and to declare a dividend.

2. To elect Directors.

3. To re-appoint the Auditors, Messrs Black, Jacques and Co. and to authorise the Directors to fix their remuneration.

By order of the Board

H. Jones

Secretary

Note: A member entitled to attend and vote may appoint a proxy to attend and vote in his stead. A proxy need not be a member of the Company.

Registered in England and Wales. No. 123456

---

21 days' notice is always required) at which only ordinary resolutions are to be considered, and a simple majority of the votes cast in favour is sufficient to pass an ordinary resolution.

Other matters will be dealt with as special resolutions, particularly the following:

change of name of the company;
alteration of Memorandum or Articles of Association.

At least 21 days' notice must be given of a general meeting at which any special resolution is to be considered and at least 75 per cent of the votes cast must be in favour for the resolution to be passed. The notice must state the terms of the resolution.

Elective resolutions are required for some special matters of fundamental importance, listed in Figure 6.2. At least 21 days' written notice must be given of a general meeting at which an elective resolution is to be considered, and the notice must state the terms of the resolution. Every member entitled to attend and vote must agree to the resolution, in person or by proxy, so this procedure is in practice likely to be of use only to companies with a few shareholders.

Remember that if a special or an elective resolution is passed a signed copy must be lodged with the Registrar of Companies within 14 days of the meeting.

Extraordinary resolutions are required only for certain purposes connected with voluntary winding-up (though occasionally the Articles may require other business to be dealt with by an extraordinary resolution). They are not dealt with further here.

Voting at general meetings

The Articles of Association will set out the voting rights of shareholders. They are usually one vote per member on a show of hands. As this may not always be fair (because members hold different numbers of shares) a poll may be demanded when there is one vote per share. Note that a director is not entitled to vote at a general meeting unless he is a shareholder.

Any member can appoint a proxy (who does not himself have to be a member) to attend and vote on his behalf on a poll. To be valid the form or letter appointing the proxy usually has to be received by the company at least 48 hours before the start of the meeting. A proxy may speak at a meeting, and has the right to demand a poll though he can vote only on a poll and not on a show of hands. The chairman usually has a casting vote. The full details of the voting entitlements and rights to demand a poll will be included in the Articles.

At meetings of small private companies, like our example Smith, Brown and Robinson Limited, there is seldom any dispute which leads to problems in dealing with the business and therefore a poll is hardly ever needed. However, if a poll is properly demanded in accordance with the Articles, it is best to distribute to each shareholder present a poll slip on which to vote – it can be based on the draft proxy form which is usually given in the Articles. These are collected, the number of votes to which each shareholder is entitled calculated by reference to the shareholding as shown in the Register of Shareholders, and the votes counted. The chairman can then declare the result of the vote.

Procedure for holding general meetings

Once the board has decided to hold a general meeting, the secretary must prepare the notice of meeting (see Figure 6.3 on page 59) and send a copy to each director, each shareholder and the auditor. A copy of the Director's Report and the accounts must also be sent to each of these people at least 21 clear days before the AGM. It is therefore usually, but not necessarily, sent with the notice of AGM. Twenty-one clear days' notice of the meeting must be given, excluding the day of posting and the day of the meeting (see also the provision in the Articles on notice). The notice must include the note informing shareholders of their rights to appoint proxies.

It is possible to convene the meeting without giving the full 21 days' notice if *all* the shareholders who are entitled to attend and vote agree. Such agreement should preferably be in writing, to avoid any later dispute. A specimen is shown in Figure 6.4 on the following page.

The secretary must book the room for the meeting and have available:

the Register of Members (in case of a poll when the number of shares owned by each member will be relevant);

the Memorandum and Articles of Association;

minutes of previous general meetings (which may be inspected by members);

a copy of the notice and the Directors' Report and Accounts;

copies of directors' service contracts and the Register of Directors' Interests (which may be inspected by members).

During the meeting the secretary should take notes of the discussion and voting, and afterwards prepare minutes, in much the same way as he does at a board meeting, as explained in Chapter 5, page 48.

Figure 6.4. *Waiver of notice for AGM*

WAIVER

WE, the undersigned being all the members of
Smith, Brown and Robinson Limited

entitled to attend and vote at the Annual General Meeting of the Company to be held in respect of the year 19XX waive our statutory rights in accordance with Sections 240 and 369 of the Companies Act 1985:

(a) to the calling of the Annual General Meeting for the year 19XX by shorter notice than the 21 days specified in Section 369;

(b) to the despatch of the Balance Sheet (including every other document required by law to be annexed thereto) to persons entitled to receive the same, less than 21 days before the date of the Annual General Meeting for 19XX (Section 240).

We also agree to the calling of any other general meeting during 19XX by shorter notice than that prescribed in Section 369 of the Companies Act 1985 and to the proposing and passing at such general meeting or at the said Annual General Meeting of any special resolution notwithstanding that less than 21 days' notice of such resolution has been given.

_____   _____

_____   _____

Date _____

CHAPTER 7

Year-end Duties

The annual tasks

The end of the financial year (the Accounting Reference Period, to give it the official title) gives rise to a number of specific tasks, and the following timetable may serve as a reminder of the various items which must be attended to at this time.

1. Check at year-end that the Registers of Directors, Members, and Directors' Interests are up to date.
2. When the accounts are being drafted, prepare the draft Directors' Report.
3. Obtain the directors' approval to the accounts and Directors' Report in preparation for signature by the auditor.
4. Obtain director's signature on three final copies of the balance sheet and secretary's signature on the Directors' Report and then obtain the signature of the auditor.
5. Fix date of AGM.
6. Issue Notice of AGM and copies of accounts and Directors' Report to shareholders (and auditors) at least 21 clear days before the meeting, unless all members have consented to short notice.
7. Prepare dividend cheques and tax vouchers, if a dividend is being recommended to the AGM.
8. Hold AGM.
9. Issue dividend cheques and tax vouchers if dividend has been approved.
10. Prepare the Annual Return.
11. Lodge the Annual Return with the Registrar of Companies.
12. Lodge the accounts and Directors' Report with the Registrar of Companies.

The timetable for year-end duties set out above may look formidable practice it is not particularly difficult. However, the should be aware that failing to comply with the nents may in some cases lay him and/or the company open enalty.

First, the time limits should be remembered. The AGM must be held once in every calendar year, and not more than 15 months after the preceding AGM. The Annual Return must be filed within 42 days of the AGM, made up as at the fourteenth day after the AGM but see also paragraph on the Annual Return on page 70. The Directors' Report and accounts must be prepared in time for copies to be filed with the Registrar of Companies not more than 10 months after the end of the financial year. If these time limits are not adhered to there may be objections from shareholders, which will have to be answered. The Registrar of Companies will send a reminder notice requiring submission of the missing documents and pointing out that penalties may be incurred in the event of continuing default.

Second, the correct procedure for convening the AGM must be followed, particularly if there are more than two or three shareholders, as otherwise dissent can be caused between them.

Descriptions of most of these items will be found elsewhere in this book but we will now deal with the Directors' Report, Statutory Accounts, Annual General Meeting and the Annual Return.

The Directors' Report

At the end of each financial year the annual accounts have to be prepared. The Companies Acts require that a Directors' Report be attached to the balance sheet in the annual accounts and be examined by the auditor as to its consistency with the financial statements.

The Report should contain:

statement of the principal activities of the company and any significant change in those activities during the year;
a fair view of the state and development of the company;
details of any important events since the year end;
an indication of likely future development of the business;
a list of the names of all persons who were directors at any time in the year;
statement of changes among the directors since the last AGM;
list of directors standing for election at the AGM;
directors' interests in shares and debentures of the company;
donations for charitable or political purposes, if they exceed £200;
reference to a number of financial matters (including any proposal to pay a dividend) on which the auditor will advise.

When the board has approved the Directors' Report and the accounts, the Report can be signed by the secretary on behalf of the board, or by one of the directors. If signed by a director it must state 'for and on behalf of the Board', and if by the secretary, 'by order of the Board'. An example of a Report is given in Figure 7.1. on pages 66–67.

After signature, the Report must be circulated to all members of the company with the accounts, and an original signed copy of both documents has to be filed with the Registrar of Companies (see below).

It is convenient here to refer to the election of directors at the AGM. The Articles of Association should be consulted but it will usually be found (and is included in Table A Articles) that at the first AGM all the directors must retire and stand for re-election. At subsequent AGMs any director appointed since the previous AGM must retire and stand for election. It is also usual for one-third of the directors to retire in rotation and stand for re-election. The precise wording of the Articles will indicate exactly how many directors have to retire; sometimes it is at least one-third, or it can be the number nearest to, but not more than one-third. Of course, if directors wish to leave the board, perhaps because of age, they do not have to stand for re-election.

If the company is a 'small company', which is a specific term defined in the Acts, it is exempted from certain requirements and may produce modified accounts for filing with the Registrar, although the members must still be sent the full Directors' Report and Accounts (though see below).

A 'small company' is one which satisfies two of the following three conditions:

(a) annual turnover must not exceed £2,000,000
(b) balance sheet total must not exceed £1,000,000 net
(c) average number of employees must not exceed 50.

The exemptions for a 'small company' are as follows:

(a) no profit and loss account need be filed
(b) no Directors' Report need be filed
(c) the balance sheet which is filed may be summarised and the notes to the accounts may be abbreviated.

Where a company takes advantage of an exemption from including an item, the modified accounts must include a statement by the directors, immediately above their signature, which states that:

(a) they have relied upon the exemption and
(b) they have done so on the grounds that the company is entitled to the benefit of that exemption.

Figure 7.1.   *Draft Directors' Report*

SMITH, BROWN AND ROBINSON LIMITED

Directors: Mr S Smith   5 West Street,
          Mrs B Brown   Newtown,
                                         England.

DIRECTORS' REPORT

The Directors have pleasure in submitting their Report, with the Accounts for the period from the date of incorporation of the Company (17th October 19XX) to 31st March 19XX.

Activities

The Company carries on business as a confectioner, tobacconist and newsagent.

Turnover

An analysis of the turnover by activity is given in note 2 to the accounts.

Results for the year

Analysis of profit before taxation is given in note 5(a) to the accounts.

Changes in Fixed Assets

There were no significant changes in the fixed assets of the Company during the period other than the acquisition of the whole of the issued share capital of White (Toys) Ltd.

Share issues

On 1st November 19XX 98 Ordinary Shares of £1 each were issued for cash at par, in addition to the two subscribers' shares issued on formation of the company, to provide funds to the company.

On 12th February 19XX the authorised capital of the company was raised to £200. On 13th February 19XX 25 ordinary shares were issued for a consideration of £625.

Figure 7.1. *Draft Directors' Report (continued)*

Dividends

The Directors recommend payment of a dividend at the rate of 10% on the issued Ordinary Shares and shareholders will be asked at the Annual General Meeting to declare this dividend.

Transfer to reserves

£1200 was transferred to revenue reserves as at 31st March 19XX.

Directors

The Directors of the Company at the end of the year are listed above, both having been appointed on 1st November 19XX. Mrs T Taylor was a director from 17th to 31st October 19XX.

Directors' Interests

The Directors were interested in the shares of the Company as follows:

	at 17th Oct 19XX	at 31st Mar 19XX
Mr S Smith	NIL	50 Ordinary Shares
Mrs B Brown	NIL	50 Ordinary Shares

By order of the Board

th	19X2	
		Secretary

Registered Office:

1 High Street,
Newtown,
England.
Registered in England and Wales.   No. 123456

If a company is dormant, that is not trading at all, it is also allowed exemption from certain requirements.

The accountant or auditor will advise on the precise details of all these exemptions.

Annual accounts

The directors are responsible for the preparation and content of the annual accounts. These comprise a profit and loss account and a balance sheet, and are produced for each accounting reference period by the accountant under the direction of the directors, for the shareholders. The general procedure for preparing the annual accounts and the Directors' Report is as follows:

Drafts will be produced by the accountant and the secretary respectively (see Figure 7.1 on page 66) and will be discussed with the directors, particularly the managing director if one has been appointed, to ensure that they are not only accurate in detail but also correctly represent the state of the company's affairs.

After the drafts have been agreed within the company they will be discussed with the auditor, who may require some corrections or changes following the audit of the account books and records. The auditor may well wish to discuss the accounts with the directors. Once the auditor is satisfied, the final version will be typed and placed before the board for approval at a formal board meeting. The board, in approving the Report and the accounts, should authorise one director to sign the balance sheet on behalf of the company. After this has been done (and at least three copies will have to be signed) the documents are sent to the auditor, who needs to be satisfied that all is in order, and who will then sign the auditor's report which will be included as an integral part of the accounts. The auditor will retain one copy and return the other two copies to the company.

It is customary for the date of the AGM to be fixed by the board when the Report and accounts are approved, so that when the auditor returns the two copies, other copies can be made and these must be sent to the shareholders with the formal notice of AGM. Each copy must show clearly the name of the director who signed the balance sheet.

One signed copy of the Report and accounts should be kept by the secretary in a safe place as a formal record. It is often convenient to keep it as an appendix to the minutes of the board or general meeting.

The third signed copy of the Report and accounts must be sent to the Registrar of Companies, usually with the Annual Return (though they can be sent separately) unless the company is a small company, as described earlier, when a special abbreviated balance sheet may be prepared, audited and then filed with the Registrar.

The time limit for filing the Report and accounts for private companies is 10 months after the end of the relevant ARP. Where the company has overseas interests, an extension of three months can be claimed by giving notice to the Registrar on Form CF242 (see the *Notes for Guidance* issued by the Registrar, for further information).

Dispensing with laying accounts

It is possible to dispense with the requirement to lay the Directors' Report and accounts before the shareholders at AGMs by passing an elective resolution. If it is desired to do this, advice should be sought from the auditor on the wording of the resolution. Note that this does not remove the requirement to prepare the Report and accounts and circulate copies to the shareholders in the usual way.

Annual General Meeting

The company must give at least 21 days' notice of the AGM unless all members agree, in writing, to waive notice. This procedure can be most useful if there are only a few shareholders. A specimen form of waiver is shown in Figure 6.4, page 62.

The notice of meeting must state:

venue,

time and date of the meeting, and

purpose of the meeting: that is, the business to be transacted; the terms of any special resolution must be set out in full.

There must also be a note to the effect that the members have the right to appoint proxies. This is shown in the specimen notice of meeting in Figure 6.3 on page 59.

The notice of meeting *must* be sent to all those entitled to attend, that is shareholders, directors and auditor. The term 'shareholders' includes holders of preference shares, though they are not usually entitled to attend unless their dividend is in arrear, or in other special circumstances, which will be spelt out in the Articles. If the company has issued debenture or loan stocks it is usually necessary to send copies of the notice to holders of those stocks, though they are not usually entitled to attend the meeting.

Special notice has to be given to the company by a member in certain circumstances relating to the appointment of the auditor (see Chapter 8, page 92).

The ordinary business which is usually dealt with at an AGM includes:

consideration and adoption of the annual accounts, Directors' Report, and Auditors' Report;
election of directors;
declaration of final dividend; and
appointment and remuneration of auditors.

Any other business would be classed as special business.

At the meeting there should be formal proposers for each resolution (strictly speaking seconders are not necessary, though it is common practice for motions to be seconded), and the chairman should allow shareholders the opportunity to raise questions on the matters being considered. Any shareholder who wishes to propose an amendment to an ordinary resolution should be allowed to do so, and the amendment should be voted upon before the resolution itself is decided. You should note that it is not permissible for a resolution to pay a dividend to be amended to increase the amount payable, though it may be reduced. No amendment may be made to a special or elective resolution. The Auditors' Report *must* be read out, not taken as read.

After the meeting the secretary should prepare the minutes, and after these have been approved in draft by the chairman, authority for their signature can be obtained at the next board meeting. A specimen set of minutes is shown in Figure 7.2.

If a dividend has been approved the secretary must arrange for the necessary cheques and tax vouchers to be prepared and sent out (see Chapter 8, page 80 for further information on the payment of dividends).

Following the AGM, the Annual Return must be prepared as this is required to show certain particulars as at 14 days after the date of the meeting. Details of this are given below.

Sometimes the Directors' Report and accounts are not ready when the time limit for holding the AGM (15 months after the previous AGM, but not later than 31 December each year) expires (even though they have to be filed with the Registrar within 10 months of the end of the ARP). In these circumstances the AGM should be held to deal with the other items and then adjourned until the accounts are ready. The adjourned meeting should be re-convened with proper notice as laid down in the Articles. Table A provides that at least seven days' notice of an adjourned meeting must be given if the adjournment is for 14 days or more. No fresh notice is needed if the date was fixed at the original meeting and is within 14 days of that meeting.

Figure 7.2. *Specimen set of AGM minutes*

SMITH, BROWN AND ROBINSON LIMITED

Minutes of the Annual General Meeting
of the Company held at 1 High Street
Newtown on 30th June 19XX

Present: Mr S Smith (in the chair)
Mrs B Brown
Mr M Brown

In Attendance: Mrs H Jones, Secretary

NOTICE OF MEETING

The Notice of Meeting was read and it was reported that all of
the members had agreed to accept short notice.

REPORT OF AUDITORS

The Report of the Auditors was read.

DIRECTORS' REPORT AND ACCOUNTS FOR THE PERIOD
ENDED 31st MARCH 19XX

The Chairman proposed – "that the Report of the Directors and
the audited accounts for the period ended 31st March 19XX now
submitted to this meeting, be and are hereby received and adopted" and that a dividend at the rate of 10 per cent be declared
payable on the ordinary shares on 1st July 19XX. Mrs Brown
seconded the resolution which was put to the meeting and
declared carried.

RE-ELECTION OF DIRECTORS

Mr Smith proposed that Mrs Brown, as a retiring Director, be
and is hereby re-elected a Director of the company.

Mrs Brown proposed that Mr Smith, as a retiring Director, be
and is hereby re-elected a Director of the company.

The resolutions were seconded, put to the meeting and
declared carried.

AUDITORS

In accordance with Section 384 of the Companies Act 1985 it
was proposed by Mrs Brown and seconded by Mr Smith and

RESOLVED that Messrs. Black, Jacques and Co. be and are
hereby reappointed auditors of the company and
that the directors be authorised to fix their
remuneration.

There being no other business the meeting was closed.

The Annual Return

The Annual Return on Form A363 must be submitted to the Registrar of Companies after the AGM. The return is effectively a copy or summary of the entries in the statutory books, and if the books are kept up to date the return will be easy to complete. It must be submitted with a fee of £25 within 42 days of the company's AGM, made up to the fourteenth day after the date of the meeting. If for some reason no AGM is held in the year (which is an offence) an Annual Return must nevertheless be prepared, made up to a date 14 days after the latest day by which the AGM should have been held (see above) or 31 December, whichever is the earlier. It is often convenient to submit the Annual Return to the Registrar at the same time as the Directors' Report and annual accounts.

In the autumn of 1990 the foregoing will be superseded by new legislation. The format of the Annual Return and requirements for lodging it will be changed and the document (which will colloquially be known as the 'shuttle document') will be initiated by the Registrar of Companies and sent to the company at its Registered Office some weeks before it is due to be submitted. Some of the information will be preprinted and this must be checked and the form amended and completed as necessary, particularly as the first issue may well be incomplete in a number of respects.

This form must then be made up to a date which is the anniversary of the date of incorporation (newly formed companies) or the anniversary of the date of the last previous return (other companies), and submitted within 28 days of that date. Failure to submit the Return on time is an offence, and the Registrar has power, which he uses if necessary, to prosecute those responsible for default.

CHAPTER 8

Special Events

This section covers a number of special events which may occur from time to time.

Shares

Transfers of shares

In time a shareholder will wish to transfer some (or perhaps all) of his or her shares to another person. To do this the shareholder must complete a Share Transfer Form and have this stamped by the Inland Revenue. It is known as an STF and may be obtained from any legal stationer. The Revenue will decide how much stamp duty has to be paid, depending on the value they place on the shares, and when this is paid, a Revenue embossed stamp will be impressed on the STF which will be returned to the person who lodged it. (The 1990 Budget proposed the abolition of stamp duty on share transfers and this is likely to become effective from late 1991–92.)

The STF must then be passed to the secretary with the share certificate covering the shares being sold. It must be checked to see that it has been completed correctly, and that the Revenue has stamped it. (It is illegal to register any transfer of shares if no stamp duty has been paid.) In particular it is wise to check that the signature is genuine, and in any case of doubt the STF should be returned to the transferor with a request that the signature be authenticated by a bank, solicitor or other reliable person. The secretary should then put the STF to a board meeting for approval of registration and issue of a new share certificate to the new shareholder. A sample board resolution is given in Figure 5.2 on page 44.

After approval by the board, the secretary must enter the details of the STF in the Register of Transfers and in the Register of

Members, making entries in the account of the shareholder who has sold the shares and in an account for the new shareholder. The old share certificate must be cancelled, and a new one prepared; this must be sealed in accordance with the usual procedure (see Chapter 8, page 85) and issued to the new shareholder. If the selling shareholder has not sold all his or her shares, but has supplied a share certificate for more shares than he has sold, he will require a balance certificate for the unsold shares. A balance certificate is produced in exactly the same way as any other share certificate, and after sealing is issued to the selling shareholder. Receipts should be obtained for all share certificates sent out. The old cancelled share certificate must be kept safely for at least a year and the STF must be kept permanently.

It should be remembered that an English company is not permitted to take notice of, or to enter in the Register of Members, information regarding any trust affecting the shares. The registered owner (the shareholder) must be regarded as the legal owner. The law in Scotland is different and trusts affecting ownership of shares are often entered in the Registers of Members of Scottish companies.

An action list which sets out the steps involved in dealing with a share transfer can be found in Figure 4.2 on page 34.

Transmission of shares

Transmission of shares occurs when a shareholder dies or is declared of unsound mind. The latter is unusual and will not be dealt with here. If you encounter this you should seek professional advice.

If a shareholder dies the shares form part of the estate. On hearing of the death the secretary should ask to see the death certificate, and should make an appropriate entry in the Register of Members. From that time any further dividends declared must be retained and not paid to the estate, until probate has been taken out or other satisfactory steps taken to clear up the deceased's affairs. The executor will also wish to know if any dividends paid previously have not been cashed, in order to find these or ask for duplicate cheques.

When probate has been granted, the secretary should ask to see a copy of the grant – this should be one of the copies issued by the Probate Registry with its impressed stamp, not just a photocopy. The secretary should note the details and the executor's name and address on the Register of Members and preferably keep a photocopy of the grant. The original should be returned to the executor who will then have to decide what he wishes to do with the shares.

There are three alternative courses of action:

to leave the shares registered in the name of the deceased with the name of the executor entered on the Register of Members;

to transfer the shares into the executor's own name; or

to transfer the shares into the name of a beneficiary of the estate.

In all cases, when the probate has been registered the secretary should pay the executor the arrears of dividends which have accumulated.

If the shares are to be left in the deceased's name there is no further action to take beyond making sure that the executor's name and address are entered accurately on the Register for correspondence and dividend purposes. If the shares are to be transferred into the name of the executor, a Letter of Request should be completed by the executor – see Figure 8.1 – and this should be registered by the secretary

Figure 8.1. *Letter of Request*

Request of Executors or Administrators to be placed on the Register.

To the Secretary, Smith, Brown and Robinson Ltd.

Name of deceased shareholder . . . .

I, the undersigned, being the Executor/Administrator of the above deceased hereby give you notice that it is my desire to be registered as proprietor of the undermentioned shares in your company in my own right as follows:

Number of shares . . . . (figures) . . . . (words)

In the name of . . . .

Address . . . .

. . . .

subject to the conditions on which the same are held at the date of this request.

Signature . . . .

Date . . . .

Note: This request must be accompanied by the appropriate share certificates.

---

in the same way as a transfer, except that no stamp duty is payable.

If the shares are to be transferred to a beneficiary, then the executors must complete an ordinary STF and the normal procedure set out above (including stamping by the Inland Revenue) should be followed.

If the total value of the deceased's estate is small, the person dealing with it may not wish to bother with taking out probate. In practice it is usual to accept this situation if the total estate is less than about £5000. The secretary should ask to see a copy of the will, and once satisfied that the estate is small, and that the executor is acting honestly and responsibly, he may accept the executor's instructions as to the shares, but should obtain a statutory declaration which has been sworn before a Commissioner of Oaths (see Figure 8.2) and the instructions in writing, with an undertaking from the executor to indemnify the company in respect of any liability it may incur if it is later discovered that a mistake has been made.

Joint shareholdings

It is quite possible for two or more people to hold shares in a company jointly, and such shareholding accounts are called joint accounts. The procedure is that the STF by which they acquire their shares will have both names (or all the names if there are more than two) in the section referring to the transferee, together with the addresses. As far as the Register of Members is concerned it is usual to record all the names, in the order in which they are shown on the STF, together with the address of the first named holder, as one account. The share certificate should list all the names.

The Articles of Association will usually have a restriction on the number of holders in a joint account (four being the usual number). Annual reports, dividends and other communications will be sent to the first named holder. Should one of the holders die his or her name is deleted when the death certificate is noted and no other change is needed (except to note a new address if the first named holder dies). When there is only one holder left, the account is dealt with in exactly the same way as any other single holder account.

The Articles of Association will set out the voting rights which apply to joint accounts. Usually the holder whose name stands first in the share register can exercise the votes attached to the shares, and in his or her absence the right moves to the next named holder and so on.

From the point of view of the joint shareholders there are a number of matters which should be taken into account affecting their personal circumstances, but these will not be dealt with in this book.

Figure 8.2. *Statutory declaration for a small estate*

The Secretary,
Smith, Brown and Robinson Limited

In the Estate of . . . . (name) late of . . . .

. . . .(address)

I do hereby solemnly declare that . . . .(name) died on

. . . . (date) and that I am the only person entitled to deal
with the Estate of the said deceased and that I will administer
according to law the Estate of the said deceased which may
come into my hands and that I will render a true and just account
thereof whenever required by law to do so and that there is no
Inheritance Tax or other duty payable in connection with the
death of the said deceased and I make this solemn declara-tion
conscientiously believing the same to be true and by virtue of
the Statutory Declarations Act, 1835.

In consideration of your accepting for registration the
Transfer/Letter of Request executed by me for the purpose of
transferring . . . .
. . . . (number of shares in words) out of the name of the
deceased without production of a Grant of Probate or
Representation, I do hereby agree to save you harmless and
keep you indemnified from and against all losses, damages,
charges, costs and expenses which you may sustain, incur or
be liable to in consequence of your so doing.

I further undertake to obtain and produce to the Company a
Grant of Probate or Representation of the Estate of the
deceased if so required by the Company.

Signature . . . .

Declared at . . . .

Before me . . . .

this . . . . day of . . . . 19 . . . . . .

Commissioner of Oaths.

Marriages and changes of name and address

From time to time a shareholder may change his or her name or address, perhaps on marriage. Provided satisfactory evidence of the change is received by the secretary, the new information should be entered in the Register of Members, indicating the date of the change. The previous information should remain on the Register as a note.

Satisfactory evidence would be the original marriage certificate or deed poll to substantiate a change of name. A copy of this document should be kept, and the original returned to the shareholder. For a change of address a signed statement from the shareholder stating both the old and new addresses should be obtained. This statement should be filed safely.

Lost certificates and dividend warrants

If a shareholder reports the loss of a share certificate or dividend warrant, the secretary should be careful. If a share certificate is missing the holder should first be asked to make a very careful search, and it is often helpful to tell the holder the date it was issued, to whom it was sent, for example the solicitor, and who signed the receipt acknowledging its delivery. If it still cannot be found then the shareholder should be asked to sign a Form of Indemnity (see the example shown in Figure 8.3) which should be countersigned by a bank which will probably charge the shareholder a fee. This action is necessary because a share certificate is prima facie a title to the shares and when two certificates are in issue for the same shares (the lost certificate and the replacement certificate), the company must be protected against the possible misuse of the lost certificate – by its use as security for a loan, or by its attempted sale at a later date when it may be found.

When the indemnity is received a duplicate certificate may be prepared, clearly marked 'Duplicate', sealed and issued. The facts of the issue should be recorded in the Register of Members. The original, lost, certificate then ceases to have any value and if it is later found, should be returned to the secretary for cancellation.

If a dividend warrant or cheque is lost, the secretary should first check that has not already been paid. If not, then a 'stop' should be placed on the warrant with the bank and a new one may be issued. Again, it is advisable to note the facts on the dividend list.

If a dividend tax voucher is lost a duplicate may be issued, but it is a requirement of the Inland Revenue that it should be marked 'Duplicate' very clearly.

Figure 8.3. *Form of indemnity for lost share certificate*

To the Secretary,
Smith, Brown and Robinson Limited

Dear Sir,

The Certificate for . . . . (number in figures) (. . . . .

(number in words)) shares of £x in your company, which were

registered in the name of . . . . having been

lost, stolen or destroyed, I request you to issue a duplicate certificate and in consideration of your so doing I hereby for myself and my legal personal representatives

(a) agree to keep you indemnified against all actions, proceedings, liability, claims, damages, costs and expenses in relation to or arising out of your so doing and to pay on demand all payments, losses, costs and expenses suffered or incurred by you in consequence thereof or arising thereout;

(b) irrevocably authorise you to make any payments and comply with any demands which may be claimed from or made upon you in consequence of your so doing without any reference to or authority from me and such payments or compliances shall be accepted by me as conclusive evidence that you are liable to make such payments or to comply with such demands on my behalf.

And I further declare that I have not in any way knowingly parted with the said document and I undertake to return the same to you should it come into my possession.

Dated this . . . . day of . . . . 19 . . . . .

Signed . . . . (shareholder)

We, the undersigned, hereby join in the above indemnity.

. . . . Bank plc

Preference shares, loan stocks and debentures
If the company has issued preference shares, loan stocks or debentures, registers of the holders must be maintained in the same way as the Register of Members. Indeed, preference shareholders are members of the company, though the rights attached to their shares will differ from those attached to ordinary shares. Transfers will be registered in accordance with the procedures set out on page 73–74 except that no stamp duty is payable on transfers of loan stocks and debentures.

Changes of director and/or secretary

Though there are occasions when a director is removed from the board (see page 91), a more common reason for a change of director or secretary is resignation or retirement. The procedure is to obtain a formal letter of resignation from the individual, submit this to the board for noting and approval of a new appointment if appropriate, and then make the entry in the Register of Directors or of Secretaries. A Company Form G288 must also be completed and sent to the Registrar of Companies notifying the change. If a director leaves a replacement may be appointed, and if the secretary leaves a replacement must be appointed, and it is convenient to notify the new appointment on the same company form as the resignation. Remember, the form must be sent to the Registrar within 14 days of the change, and details of the new appointment must also be entered in the appropriate Register.

Action lists which serve both as a reminder and a note of action taken are given on pages 52, 53 and 91–2.

Dividends

If the company is trading profitably shareholders can expect to obtain an income from their shares by way of dividends, but a company may make a distribution only from net realised profits. These are accumulated realised profits less accumulated realised losses of either a capital or revenue nature. These terms can be explained as follows, though a detailed definition is best obtained from an accountant. Accumulated means including amounts brought forward from a previous ARP. Realised means actually obtained from completed transactions, not merely expected. Capital means relating to the fixed assets of the business. Revenue means relating to the normal manufacturing, purchasing or selling activities of the business. In summary, the profits must have been achieved before they can be paid out as dividends (unlike interest, which is a liability of the company whether profits are made or not).

Interim and final dividends

The board may either:

declare an interim dividend – this often happens part of the way through the financial year if trade is good, and/or
recommend that the shareholders approve a final dividend at the AGM.

When the decision has been taken the secretary arranges preparation of the cheques (often called 'dividend warrants') for the amount due to each shareholder. A covering letter must also be provided, often called a tax voucher or voucher, which certifies the tax credit to which each shareholder is entitled (see Figure 8.4).

Tax credits

A tax credit arises because every time the company makes a payment of dividend, it incurs a liability to pay in advance part of the corporation tax which will eventually be due on its profits. This advance corporation tax (known as ACT) has to be paid over to the Inland Revenue and is retained by them even if there is no liability to pay any corporation tax when the tax computation is later agreed. The amount due as ACT is related to the rate of basic rate of income tax – when this is 25 per cent of the ACT, and hence the tax credit for the shareholders, is 25/75 of the amount of dividend paid.

In practice if a shareholder is to receive a dividend of £75, he is sent a cheque for £75 with a tax voucher, in the terms shown in the example. The company will later have to account to the Inland Revenue for the £25 ACT, but may set this off against any corporation tax liability it may have later.

After payment of the dividend, arrangements must be made for payment of the ACT to the Collector of Taxes.

Interest payments on loan stock and debentures are dealt with in much the same way, except that income tax must be deducted from the gross payment, the net amount of interest paid to the stockholder and the income tax paid to the Inland Revenue. The tax voucher then certifies the amount of tax deducted and that the company will pay the tax to the Revenue.

Registration of charges

A company is required to keep a Register of Charges, that is of mortgages and other formal pledges of its assets against debts and borrowings. When such a mortgage or borrowing is entered into, the relevant details must be entered in the Register of Charges, and in most cases it will also be necessary to deliver the document

Figure 8.4.   *Dividend tax voucher*

SMITH, BROWN AND ROBINSON LIMITED

Directors: Mrs B Brown   1 High Street,
                 S Smith   Newtown NE8 1AX
                                                    2nd July 19XX

Dear Mr Smith

Dividend for the period ending
31st March 19XX

I give below the details of the dividend payment made to you on 1st July 19XX.

No. shares: 40 ordinary shares of £1

Dividend rate: 10%

Dividend for the period ending 31st March, 19X2: £4.00

Tax Credit: £1.33

It is hereby certified that Advance Corporation Tax of an amount equal to the tax credit shown above will be accounted for to the Collector of Taxes.

Yours faithfully,
for Smith, Brown and Robinson Limited

H. Jones

H. Jones
Secretary

Mr S Smith,
12 The Avenue,
Newtown.

Company No. 123456   Registered in England and Wales
Registered Office: 1 High Street, Newtown, England.

creating the charge together with the relevant form (usually Form M395) to the Registrar for registration *within 21 days*. Frequently the other party – for example a bank – will arrange to notify the Registrar, because if the charge is not notified within the 21 days, then the other party cannot rely on it if the company becomes insolvent.

The secretary will not often be required to deal with this particular item of secretarial practice: a solicitor is usually involved in arranging the transaction and will advise on the precise steps to be taken.

When the charge has been satisfied (that is, the debt has been paid off) a Declaration of Satisfaction (Form M403) may be filed so that the public file of the company no longer shows the charge as extant.

Change of company name

A company may change its name to any other name subject to the general restrictions on choice of name set out in Chapter 3, page 16.

The procedure is for the board to resolve to change the name and to authorise the secretary to convene an EGM of the shareholders (unless it is convenient to deal with the matter at the next AGM). The resolution is a special resolution (see Chapter 6, page 58) and the procedure for the meeting is set out in that chapter. At the meeting the chairman must be asked to sign some copies of the resolution, four to six copies being a convenient number (see Figure 8.5). After the meeting one copy of the signed resolution must be sent to the Registrar with the fee of £40. After a short time the Registrar will issue a new Certificate of Incorporation on Change of Name, and from the date of that certificate the new name must be used.

The secretary must remember to have ordered new stationery, or at least labels or overprinting on existing stationery, a new seal, new cheque books and new name plates for display at the places of business. It is not permissible to use the old name of the company after the date of the change. Notification of the change should be sent to all companies and individuals with whom the company has dealings. It is not necessary to replace all the issued share certificates, but the new name must appear on all those issued after the date of the change.

Alteration of Memorandum and Articles of Association

Occasionally a company may wish to change the objects clause of its Memorandum of Association. This is permitted, a special resolution

Figure 8.5. *Resolution for change of company name*

Company No. 123456

THE COMPANIES ACTS 1985–1989

COMPANY LIMITED BY SHARES

SPECIAL RESOLUTION

OF

SMITH, BROWN AND ROBINSON LIMITED

Passed on Monday 00th August, 19XX

At an Extraordinary General Meeting of the above named Company, duly convened and held at . . . .
. . . . on . . . . day 00th August, 19XX at 10.00 am the following Resolution was duly passed as a Special Resolution.

RESOLUTION

THAT the name of the Company be and is hereby changed
to (New name) Limited.

_____
CHAIRMAN

---

being necessary. See also references to the objects clause in the section entitled 'The Memorandum of Association' on page 18. More frequently it may be desired to alter the Articles of Association, perhaps to increase the permitted number of directors, or to update the Articles to bring them into line with the most modern practice (which seems to change every few years). The procedure is the same in both cases.

First the exact wording of the proposed change should be drafted and it is usually desirable to consult a solicitor on this. Once this is settled, the board must formally approve the proposals, and authorise the convening of an EGM (or include the business on the agenda for the next AGM). The meeting will be convened in the usual way and the resolution dealing with the changes will be dealt with as a special resolution. The chairman must be asked to sign about six copies of the resolution and one must be sent to the Registrar of Companies within 15 days of the meeting. Unlike a change of name, the alterations are effective immediately they are passed.

The secretary must also arrange for one complete copy of the Memorandum and/or Articles to be amended and sent to the Registrar with the signed copy of the resolution. The secretary should also keep at least one amended copy for his formal records. Copies of the resolution should be sent to all holders of copies of the Memorandum and Articles of Association. If the alteration is minor (perhaps only a change of a figure or a word or two) the updated copy may be marked up in typescript, but if the alteration is more than this, the document, or at least the page, will have to be reprinted or retyped.

Sealing of documents

The company seal has been described in Chapter 3, page 20 and its use will be referred to in the Articles of Association. Generally the secretary will keep the seal in a safe place so that it may not be applied to documents by unauthorised persons, and it may well have a locking device, the key of which may be kept by the secretary or a director. When a document has to be sealed, such as a share certificate or lease, the secretary should obtain the formal approval of the board and then affix the seal in the presence of two directors or a director and himself. Both individuals should sign beside the die impression. The following wording is often used:

The Common Seal of Smith, Brown and Robinson Ltd was hereunto affixed in the presence of

Director

Secretary

A record of the sealing should be entered in the Register of Sealings, if one is kept, or made in some other manner. As mentioned previously, it is no longer necessary to have a seal and documents may be signed formally by two directors, or a director and the secretary, on behalf of the company. It is desirable to maintain a record of such documents, and they may be entered in the Register of Sealings for this purpose. The authority of the board should be obtained in all cases.

Strictly speaking, it is not in order to seal a document before obtaining board approval, but if the secretary knows that the board has approved the underlying transaction, and the director involved is agreeable, this may be done and the board asked to ratify the action taken after the event. The secretary should use discretion in such cases.

Increase of authorised capital

If the company wishes to ask its shareholders to provide more funds, or perhaps wishes to buy another business satisfying the purchase price by issue of shares rather than in cash, it will probably need to increase its authorised capital.

It is necessary to obtain board approval for an increase, and to convene an EGM. The usual procedure for this on page 58 should be followed. Copies of the ordinary resolution (see Figure 8.6) should be available for the chairman of the EGM to sign immediately after the meeting and one copy of the signed resolution must be sent to the Registrar of Companies within 15 days together with Company Form G123 (Notice of Increase in Nominal Capital). No fee or duty is payable at this stage, although of course capital duty will be payable when any of the shares are issued.

Copies of the resolution should be sent to all holders of copies of the Memorandum and Articles.

The draft resolution also includes authority to issue the shares, as described in the next section.

Issue of shares

It will no doubt be necessary at some time to issue more shares. The issue of shares is the means by which the company raises capital

Figure 8.6. *Resolution for increase of capital*

Company No. 123456

THE COMPANIES ACTS 1985–1989

COMPANY LIMITED BY SHARES

SPECIAL RESOLUTION OF

SMITH, BROWN AND ROBINSON LIMITED

Passed on Monday 00th August, 19XX

At an Extraordinary General Meeting of the above named company, duly convened and held at . . . . on Monday 00th August, 19XX the following resolution was duly passed as an ordinary resolution:

RESOLUTION

That   (a) the authorised share capital of the company be increased from £100 to £1000 by the creation of 900 ordinary shares of £1 each.

    (b) for the purpose of Section 95 of the Companies Act 1985 (and so that expressions used in this resolution shall bear the same meanings as in the said section):

      (i) the directors be and are hereby generally and unconditionally authorised to allot relevant securities up to a maximum nominal amount of £900 to such persons at such times and on such terms as they think proper during the period expiring at the end of five years from the date of this resolution; and

     (ii) the company be and is hereby authorised to make prior to the expiry of the said period any offer or agreement which would or might require relevant securities to be allotted after the expiry of the said period and the directors may allot relevant securities in pursuance of any such offer or agreement notwithstanding the expiry of any authority given by this Resolution.

. . . .
Chairman

---

with which to carry on the business, without having any liability to repay that capital to those who provide it. This is the 'risk capital' or 'equity' and is the total amount of the liability which falls on the shareholders if the company fails in its business – hence the concept of 'limited liability' which is provided by operating through a company. First, the secretary must check that the company has unissued shares, that is that the authorised capital exceeds the issued capital. If not, the authorised capital will first have to be increased as set out above.

As an example we will assume that our company, Smith, Brown and Robinson Ltd, wishes to issue the 98 unissued shares. However, there is legislation regarding the issue of shares. The directors can allot shares only if:

(a) in the first five years from the date of incorporation authority is given in the Articles of Association, or
(b) the members give the directors authority to allot shares (see wording in resolution for increase of capital in Figure 8.6).

This authority must now be renewed every five years though there are provisions whereby the authority can be given for an indefinite period. An elective resolution is required and professional advice should be sought on the wording of the resolution if it is desired to do this.

Shares being issued for cash must also be offered first to existing members in proportion to their existing shareholdings as a 'rights' issue, unless the members or the Articles give the directors specific authority to do otherwise. This does not apply to issues of shares for a consideration other than cash. Note that it is illegal to give any financial assistance to anyone for the purchase of its own shares.

We will take the simple case that authority to allot is given in the Articles of Association. A board meeting will have to be summoned (this can be incorporated in the first board meeting proceedings if it is desired to make the issue at that time) to receive applications from the people who wish to subscribe for the new shares – let us assume it is the present two shareholders who have acquired the subscribers' shares. A specimen application letter is shown in Figure 8.7. These applications should be accompanied by cheques for the amounts involved – £49 in each case in our example – and the board will resolve to accept the applications, allot the shares and authorise the issue of share certificates under the seal of the company. A specimen board resolution is shown in Figure 5.2 on page 44.

Following the board meeting the secretary must take the following action:

Figure 8.7. *Application letter for allotment of shares*

To: The Directors
Smith, Brown and Robinson Limited
1 High Street
Newtown
NE8 1AX.

    I enclose a cheque for £49 being payment in full for 49 shares of £1 each in Smith, Brown and Robinson Limited and I hereby apply for and request you to allot such shares to me.

    I agree to take the said shares subject to the Memorandum and Articles of Association of the company and I authorise you to enter my name in the Register of Members as the holder of the said shares.

Dated this 1st day of November 19XX

Signature: *B. Brown*

Name in full: Barbara Brown

Address: 10 Low Road, Newtown

    enter up the Register of Allotments in the statutory books;
    enter up the Register of Members;
    write out the two share certificates, and affix the seal;
    notify the Registrar of Companies on Form PUC2 of the issue of
        the shares.

The company will have to pay capital duty to the Registrar, at £1 per £100 (or part of £100), on whichever of the following is greater:

(a) the total nominal value of the allotted shares, or
(b) the total amount due or payable for the shares.

These two figures are the same in our case (£98) so a cheque for £1 will have to be sent with the Form PUC2.

    The two cheques for £49 from the subscribers will be paid into the company's bank account. The new share certificates should then be sent to the two shareholders.

If the company wishes to issue more shares, then an increase in its authorised capital will be necessary, and the procedure for this is set out in detail above.

If the Articles do not give the directors authority to allot shares then a general meeting must be convened to approve the issue – see paragraph (b) of the resolution in Figure 8.6 on page 87. Further, if the new shares are being issued for cash, but are not being offered to existing members in proportion to their holdings (as a rights issue) the members in general meeting must approve the issue. This is because the Companies Act gives existing members pre-emptive rights to take up shares in proportion to their existing holdings whenever shares are issued for cash, unless those members agree otherwise.

The wording for a draft resolution is shown in Figure 8.8. When passed, a signed copy must be sent to the Registrar.

Figure 8.8.   *Resolution for disapplication of pre-emption rights*

Special Resolution

That the Directors be and they are hereby generally authorised in accordance with the provisions of Section 95 of the Companies Act 1985 to allot equity securities (and to make any offer or agreement which would or might require equity securities to be allotted) within the terms of their existing general authority as if Section 89(1) of the Companies Act 1985 did not apply to any such allotment subject to the terms of the restrictions and provisions following namely

(a) this authorisation shall be limited to the allotment of equity securities up to an aggregate nominal value of £ . . . .

(b) this authorisation shall (unless previously revoked or varied) expire on . . . . (date not more than five years from date of resolution)

(c) the expression 'equity securities' shall bear the same meaning in this resolution as in Section 94 of the Companies Act 1985.

Figure 8.9. *Resignation of director*

DIRECTOR'S RESIGNATION

NAME . . . .

DATE OF RESIGNATION . . . .

	Action taken (Date)
1. Board resolution	. . . .
2. Notify Registrar of Companies (within 14 days) Form G288	. . . .
3. Notify bankers if authorised signatory	. . . .
4. Enter up Register of Directors	. . . .
5. Enter up Register of Directors' Holdings	. . . .

Terminating the appointment of a director

It sometimes happens that members of a board of directors fall out and there is no way out of the situation except for one (or more) of them to leave the company. If the director is prepared to resign there is no problem and the resignation will be accepted. The appropriate board resolution noting the resignation should be passed and the Form G288 sent to the Registrar. An action list for the resignation of a director is given in Figure 8.9.

However, if the director concerned will not resign, a special procedure will have to be followed to terminate his appointment. This procedure will be laid down in the Articles but usually involves calling an EGM at which an ordinary resolution is proposed terminating the appointment of the individual concerned. Special notice of the intention to propose the resolution must be given to the company. This means that a shareholder must formally lodge with the company 28 days' notice of his intention to propose the resolution (see Figure 8.10). Copies of the special notice must be circulated to shareholders with the notice of the EGM. The resolution has to be put to the vote at the meeting, and a poll will

Figure 8.10.   *Special notice*

To The Directors,
   Smith, Brown and Robinson Limited,   (Date)

   I hereby give special notice under Sections 379 and 388 of the Companies Act 1985 of my intention to move the following ordinary resolution at the Annual General Meeting (or Extraordinary General Meeting) of the company to be held on (date) ....

(Then set out the terms of the resolution, ie to terminate the appointment of a director or to appoint new auditors.)

                      ....
                      Signature of Shareholder

probably be demanded. Whichever side is able to persuade a majority of the shareholders to support it will win the vote. The losing director has to go, and there is often some ill-feeling.

To protect the company it is necessary to follow exactly the statutory requirements relating to this situation and it is wise to seek legal advice. Subsequently the Form G288 has to be completed in the usual way, and the entry made in the Register of Directors.

Change of auditors

The auditors are appointed by the shareholders and it is part of the normal business of an AGM to reappoint the existing auditors to serve until the next AGM at which accounts are laid before the shareholders. However, if for any reason it is desired to change the auditors, and appoint a new firm, it will first be necessary to obtain the agreement of the new firm (who will probably check with the outgoing auditors the reason for the change, and any other circumstances about which they should know). The existing auditors should also be asked whether they are prepared to resign.

A special notice must be lodged with the company by a shareholder giving 28 days' notice of his intention to propose the appointment of an auditor if the proposed auditor is not also the retiring auditor, or if the retiring auditor was appointed by the directors to fill a casual vacancy, or if it is intended that an auditor be removed (see Figure 8.10 above). Copies of the special notice should be sent out with the notice of AGM and to the retiring auditor and the proposed new auditor. Retiring auditors are also entitled to have a statement circulated to the shareholders putting their case. At the AGM an ordinary resolution for the new appointment will be put to the meeting.

Sometimes an auditor expresses a wish to retire, perhaps because of giving up practice, and may send the directors a letter of resignation. This must include either a statement that there are no circumstances connected with the resignation which the auditor considers should be brought to the notice of the members or creditors of the company or a statement of such circumstances. Should a statement of the second type be necessary, the letter will have to be sent to the members or creditors, as appropriate. In any event a copy of the letter of resignation (with any statement regarding circumstances which should be brought to the notice of members), should be sent to the Registrar of Companies within 14 days of receipt. In such circumstances the directors will accept the resignation and may make a new appointment until the next AGM. At that AGM the new auditor will be appointed by the shareholders, but although at that point the auditor is the retiring auditor, there is need for the special notice from a shareholder as set out in the previous paragraph because this auditor has not been previously appointed by the shareholders, but by the directors.

After the AGM copies of the resolution appointing the new auditor, and the special notice from the shareholder, have to be sent to the Registrar of Companies.

Nominee shareholdings in subsidiary companies

If one company acquires the shares of another (perhaps because it has bought another business which was itself a company), it will have acquired a subsidiary company and itself becomes a parent company. Apart from certain accounting considerations which this entails, the company secretarial functions for the newly acquired company will be the same as, and in addition to, those of the acquiring company.

The main point to be mentioned is that a company is not permitted to have only one shareholder. Therefore, although all the shares of the subsidiary company may be owned by the parent company, they cannot all be registered in the parent company's name. It is therefore common practice to have one or two of the shares registered in the names of the directors, either in their sole names or jointly in their names and the parent company's name. This is achieved by preparing STFs to effect the transfers to the

Figure 8.11. *Declaration of trust for nominee share*

(50p stamp
to be
impressed
here)

I, ...

of . . . .

hereby acknowledge that the one share in . . . . Ltd

which is registered in my name, is held by me as nominee and in

trust for (name of parent company) . . . .

(hereinafter called "The Company") and I hereby undertake:

(a) That, on demand, I will transfer the said share to The
Company or as it shall direct
(b) That I will use the vote attaching to the said share as The
Company shall from time to time direct
(c) That I will pay over to The Company or its agents all
dividends that I may receive in respect of the said share.

I hereby authorise The Company to complete the attached
transfer in respect of the said share.
IN WITNESS whereof I have hereunto set my hand and seal this

. . . . day of . . . . One thousand nine hundred and . . . .

SIGNED SEALED AND DELIVERED
by the above named

in the presence of:-
(witness's name, address and signature)

directors, and following through the standard procedure for registering transfers of shares. The STFs will attract only a nominal stamp duty of 50p, as no beneficial interest in those shares is passing. To ensure that the present company's ownership can be made evident and protected, the nominee shareholder (as the individual holders are called) should be asked to complete a simple Declaration of Trust (see the example in Figure 8.11) and to sign an STF, the name of the transferee being omitted until it is desired to transfer the share into the name of another nominee. The STF and the Declaration of Trust should be kept safely with the share certificate for the share concerned by the secretary of the parent company.

CHAPTER 9

Terminating a Company

One of the advantages of a limited company is that it does not die. However, there are occasions when it is desired to bring a company's existence to an end. It may be that it has become insolvent, or no longer trades, having sold its business, or because the shareholders (the owners) wish to take possession of the assets, rather than hold shares.

Briefly, the company may be wound up at the request of the creditors (compulsory or creditors' liquidation), of the directors and shareholders (voluntary liquidation), or in certain circumstances the Registrar of Companies may be willing to strike off the company.

The procedures involved in winding up a company are complicated and it will be necessary for professional help to be sought.

If the company is no longer serving any useful purpose (perhaps because its business has come to an end) and it has no debts outstanding it is possible to ask the Registrar of Companies to strike it off the register. The procedure is for the directors and the secretary to resign and for a letter to be sent to the Registrar with the Form G288 which has to be lodged to notify the resignations. This letter should indicate that it is desired that the company should be struck off the register on the basis that it is no longer in business or operation. The Registrar needs to be satisfied that the facts are as stated (and in particular will enquire of the Inland Revenue to check if there is any tax unpaid) and then puts in hand the striking off procedure. It is possible for any creditor or other person having an interest of any kind in the company to object and the Registrar will not strike off the company until any such objection is resolved.

APPENDIX

Commonly Used Company Forms

The forms are Crown copyright.
Reproduced with the permission of the Controller of Her Majesty's
Stationery Office.

G

COMPANIES FORM No. 123

Notice of increase in nominal capital

123

Pursuant to section 123 of the Companies Act 1985

Please complete
legibly, preferably
in black type, or
bold block lettering

To the Registrar of Companies

For official use

Company number

Name of company

* insert full name
of company

•

gives notice in accordance with section 123 of the above Act that by resolution of the company

dated _____the nominal capital of the company has been

increased by £ _____ beyond the registered capital of £ _____.

§ the copy must be
printed or in some
other form approved
by the registrar

A copy of the resolution authorising the increase is attached.§

The conditions (eg. voting rights, dividend rights, winding-up rights etc.) subject to which the new

shares have been or are to be issued are as follow:

Please tick here if
continued overleaf

* delete as
appropriate

Signed   [Director][Secretary]† Date

Presentor's name address and
reference (if any):

For official Use

General Section   Post room

G

COMPANIES FORM No. 224

Notice of accounting reference date (to be delivered within 9 months of incorporation)

224

Pursuant to section 224 of the Companies Act 1985
as inserted by section 3 of the Companies Act 1989

Please complete
legibly, preferably
in black type, or
bold block lettering

To the Registrar of Companies
(Address overleaf)

Company number

Name of company

* insert full name
of company

*

gives notice that the date on which the company's accounting reference period is to be treated as

coming to an end in each successive year is as shown below:

Important
The accounting
reference date to
be entered along-
side should be
completed as in the
following examples:

Day   Month

5 April
Day   Month

| 0 | 5 | 0 | 4 |

30 June
Day   Month

| 3 | 0 | 0 | 6 |

31 December
Day   Month

| 3 | 1 | 1 | 2 |

‡ Insert
Director,
Secretary,
Administrator,
Administrative
Receiver or
Receiver
(Scotland) as
appropriate

Signed   Designation‡   Date

Presentor's name address
telephone number and reference (if any):

For official use
D.E.B.   Post room

G

COMPANIES FORM No. 225(1)

Notice of new accounting reference date given during the course of an accounting reference period

225(1)

Pursuant to section 225(1) of the Companies Act 1985
as inserted by section 3 of the Companies Act 1989

1. To the Registrar of Companies
   (Address overleaf - Note 6)   Company number

Name of company

•

2. gives notice that the company's new accounting reference
   date on which the current accounting reference period   Day   Month
   and each subsequent accounting reference period of
   the company is to be treated as coming, or as having
   come, to an end is

3. The current accounting reference period of the company   Day   Month   Year
   is to be treated as [shortened][extended]† and [is to be
   treated as having come to an end][will come to an end]† on

4. If this notice states that the current accounting reference period of the company is to be extended, and

   reliance is being placed on the exception in paragraph (a) in the second part of section 225(4) of the

   Companies Act 1985, the following statement should be completed:

   The company is a [subsidiary][parent]† undertaking of

   _____, company number _____

   the accounting reference date of which is _____

5. If this notice is being given by a company which is subject to an administration order and this notice

   states that the current accounting reference period of the company is to be extended AND it is to be

   extended beyond 18 months OR reliance is not being placed on the second part of section 225(4) of

   the Companies Act 1985, the following statement should be completed:

   An administration order was made in relation to the company on _____

   and it is still in force.

6. Signed   Designation‡   Date

   Presenter's name address   For official use
   telephone number and reference (if any):   D.E.B.   Post room

Form G225(1) continued

Notes

1 All references in this form to section 225 of the Companies Act 1985 is to that section as inserted by section 3 of the Companies Act 1989.

2 Under section 225(1) of the Companies Act 1985, at any time during one of its accounting reference periods a company can give notice to the registrar of companies specifying a new date ("the new accounting reference date") on which that period is to be treated as coming to an end (or, alternatively, is to be treated as having come to an end), and on which subsequent accounting reference periods are also to be treated as coming to an end. The day and month specified in the notice must be the same for both the accounting reference date and the end of the accounting reference period.

3 The notice can shorten the current accounting reference period. But, unless the company is subject to an administration order or unless the Secretary of State directs otherwise, a notice can extend a current accounting reference period only if EITHER
(a) the company giving the notice is a subsidiary undertaking or parent undertaking of another company, and the new accounting reference date coincides with the accounting reference date of the other company, or

(b) no previous accounting reference period of the company has been extended by virtue of a previous notice given by the company under section 225, or

(c) the notice is given not less than 5 years after the date on which any earlier accounting reference period of the company which was so extended came to an end.

4 Unless the company is subject to an administration order, a current accounting reference period cannot be extended so as to make it longer than 18 months.

5 The date shown in the boxes on the form should be completed in the manner shown below.

Day   Month

| 0 | 5 | 0 | 4 |

Day   Month   Year

| 0 | 5 | 0 | 4 | 1 | 9 | 8 | 5 |

6 The address for companies registered in England and Wales or Wales is:

The Registrar of Companies
Companies House
Crown Way
Cardiff
CF4 3UZ

or, for companies registered in Scotland:

The Registrar of Companies
Companies House
100-102 George Street
Edinburgh
EH2 3DJ

G

COMPANIES FORM No. 287

Notice of change in situation of registered office

287

Please do not write in this margin

Pursuant to section 287 of the Companies Act 1985

Please complete legibly, preferably in black type, or bold block lettering

To the Registrar of Companies

For official use

Company number

Name of company

* insert full name of company

gives notice that the situation of the registered office of the company has been changed to:

Postcode

† delete as appropriate

Signed   [Director][Secretary]† Date

Presentor's name address and reference (if any):

For official Use
General Section   Post room

COMPANIES FORM No. 363

Annual return
of a company

363

Pursuant to sections 363 and 364 of the Companies Act 1985

Please do not
write in
this margin

Note The appropriate fee should accompany this form

Please complete
legibly, preferably
in black type, or
bold block lettering

To the Registrar of Companies

For official use   Company number

* insert full name
of company

Annual return of (note 1)

*

† if the company has a
share capital, this
date must be the
14th day after the
annual general
meeting

The information in this return is as at

19   †.(The date of this return note 1)

Address of registered office of the company

Postcode

Total amount of indebtedness of the company
in respect of mortgages and charges
(note 2)

£

If different from the
registered office, state
address where the register
of members or any register
of debenture holders or
any duplicate or part of any
register of debentures is
kept or may be inspected.

Register of members

Register of debenture holders

Particulars of the secretary

Name (notes 3 and 4)

Previous name(s)(note 3)

Address (notes 4 and 5)

Postcode

‡ only pages 1 and 2
need be completed
in the case of a
company without
share capital

We certify this return which comprises pages 1, 2, [3, 4, 5 and 6]‡ [plus§ _____ continuation sheets]

§ enter number of
continuation sheets
attached

Signed   Director, and   Secretary

Presentor's name address and
reference (if any):

For official Use
General Section   Post room

Form G363 continued

Particulars of the director(s) of the company (notes 6 and 7)

Name (note 3)	Business Occupation
Previous name(s)(note 3)	Nationality
Address(note 5)	
Postcode	Date of birth(note 9)
Other relevant past or present directorships* (note 8)	

Name(note 3)	Business Occupation
Previous name(s)(note 3)	Nationality
Address(note 5)	
Postcode	Date of birth(note 9)
Other relevant past or present directorships* (note 8)	

Name(note 3)	Business Occupation
Previous name(s)(note 3)	Nationality
Address(note 5)	
Postcode	Date of birth(note 9)
Other relevant past or present directorships* (note 8)	

Name(note 3)	Business Occupation
Previous name(s)(note 3)	Nationality
Address(note 5)	
Postcode	Date of birth(note 9)
Other relevant past or present directorships* (note 8)	

Page 2

Note. Form 363 will be revised in autumn 1990.

Form G363 continued

Summary of share capital and debentures

Nominal share capital   £ _____

	Number of shares	Class	Nominal value of each share
divided into:- 1			£
2			£
3			£

Issued share capital and debentures

		Number	Class
1.Number of shares of each class taken up to the date of this return.	1		
	2		
	3		
2.Number of shares of each class issued subject to payment wholly in cash	1		
	2		
	3		
3.Number of shares of each class issued as fully paid up for a consideration other than cash	1		
	2		
	3		

		Amount per share	
4.Number of shares of each class issued as partly paid up for a consideration other than cash and extent to which each such share is so paid up	1	£	
	2	£	
	3	£	
5.Number of shares (if any) of each class issued at a discount	1		
	2		
	3		

Continued on page 4

LIST OF PAST

Folio in register ledger containing particulars	Names and Addresses	
		1
		2
		3
		4
		5
		6
		7
		8
		9
		10
		11
		12
		13
		14
		15

Form G363 continued

Please do not write in this margin

Please complete legibly, preferably block type, or bold block lettering

Summary of share capital and debentures continued

	Amount	Number	Class
6 Amount of discount on the issue of shares which has not been written off at the date of this return	£		
7 Amount per share called up on number of shares of each class	£		1
	£		2
	£		3
8 Total amount of calls received (note 10)	£		
9 Total amount (if any) agreed to be considered as paid on number of shares of each class issued as fully paid up for a consideration other than cash	£		1
	£		2
	£		3
10 Total amount (if any) agreed to be considered as paid on number of shares of each class issued as partly paid up for a consideration other than cash	£		1
	£		2
	£		3
11 Total amount of calls unpaid	£		
12 Total amount of sums (if any) paid by way of commission in respect of any shares or debentures	£		
13 Total amount of the sums (if any) allowed by way of discount for any debentures since the date of the last return	£		
14 Total number of shares of each class forfeited			1
			2
			3
15 Total amount paid (if any) on shares forfeited	£		
16 Total amount of shares for which share warrants to bearer are outstanding	£		
17 Total amount of share warrants to bearer issued and ISSUED	£		
surrendered respectively since the date of the last return SURRENDERED	£		
18 Number of shares comprised in each share warrant to bearer, specifying in the case of warrants of different kinds, particulars of each kind			

AND PRESENT MEMBERS (notes 11 and 12)

	Account of Shares			
Number of shares or amount of stock held by existing members at date of return (note 11)	Particulars of shares transferred since the date of the last return, or, in the case of the first return, of the incorporation of the company, by (a) persons who are still members, and (b) persons who have ceased to be members (note 12)			Remarks
	Number	Date of Registration of transfer (a)	(b)	
				1
				2
				3
				4
				5
				6
				7
				8
				9
				10
				11
				12
				13
				14
				15

Form G363 continued

LIST OF PAST

Folio in register ledger containing Particulars	Names and addresses	
		16
		17
		18
		19
		20
		21
		22
		23
		24
		25
		26
		27
		28
		29
		30

Notes

1. An annual return is required for every calendar year. If the company has a share capital the date of this return must be the 14th day after the date of the annual general meeting. If it does not have a share capital the date of this return must be a date not more than 42 days after the annual general meeting.

2. This section should include only indebtedness in respect of charges (whenever created) of any description set out in section 396(1) of the Companies Act 1985 (in the case of English and Welsh companies) or section 410(4) of that Act (in the case of Scottish companies).

3. For an individual, his present christian name(s) and surname must be given, together with any previous christian name(s) or surname(s).

   "Christian name" includes a forename. In the case of a peer or person usually known by a title different from his surname, "surname" means that title. In the case of a corporation, its corporate name must be given.

   A previous christian name or surname need not be given if: —

   (a) in the case of a married woman, it was a name by which she was known before her marriage; or

   (b) it was changed or ceased to be used at least 20 years ago, or before the person who previously used it reached the age of 18; or

   (c) in the case of a peer or a person usually known by a British title different from his surname, it was a name by which he was known before he adopted the title or succeeded to it

4. Where all the partners in a firm are joint secretaries, only the firm name and its principal office need be given.

   Where the secretary or one of the joint secretaries is a Scottish firm, give only the firm name and its principal office.

5. Usual residential address must be given. In the case of a corporation, give the registered or principal office.

6. Director includes any person who occupies the position of a director, by whatever name called, and any person in accordance with whose directions or instructions the directors of the company are accustomed to act.

7. If the space provided for listing directors is inadequate, a prescribed continuation sheet must be used.

8. The names must be given of all bodies corporate incorporated in Great Britain of which the director is also a director, or has been a director at any time during the preceeding five years.

   However a present or past directorship need not be disclosed if it is, or has been, held in a body corporate which, throughout that directorship, has been: —

   (a) a dormant company (which is a company which has had no transactions required to be entered in the company's accounting records, except any which may have arisen from the taking of shares in the company by a subscriber to the memorandum as such).

   (b) a body corporate of which the company making the return was a wholly-owned subsidiary;

Form G363 continued

AND PRESENT MEMBERS Continued (notes 11 and 12)

Number of shares or amount of stock held by existing members at date of return (note 11)	Particulars of shares transferred since the date of the last return, or, in the case of the first return, of the incorporation of the company, by (a) persons who are still members, and (b) persons who have ceased to be members (note 12)		Remarks
	Number	Date of Registration of transfer (a) (b)	
				16
				17
				18
				19
				20
				21
				22
				23
				24
				25
				26
				27
				28
				29
				30

Account of Shares

(c) a wholly-owned subsidiary of the company making the return; or

(d) a wholly-owned subsidiary of a body corporate of which the company making the return was also a wholly owned subsidiary.

9. Dates of birth need only be given if the company making the return is:—

    (a) a public company;
    (b) the subsidiary of a public company; or
    (c) the subsidiary of a public company registered in Northern Ireland

10. Include payments on application and allotment, and any sums received or shares forfeited.

11. Show all the persons currently holding shares or stock in the company at the date of the return, giving their names and addresses, the number of shares or amount of stock held, and details of all transfers since the last return or, if this is the first annual return of the company, all transfers since the company was incorporated. If more than one class of share is held please add more columns as appropriate.

Additionally, show all persons and their relevant details if they have ceased to be members since the last return was made, or if this is the first return, since the company was incorporated.

If the list of members is not in alphabetical order, an index which will enable any member to be readily located within the list must be attached to this return. If the space provided for listing members is inadequate, a prescribed continuation sheet is available.

If full details have been given on the return for either of the last two years, a company may, if it so wishes, only include in this section details relating to persons who since the date of the last return:
    (a) have become members;
    (b) have ceased to be members; or
    (c) are existing members whose holdings of stock or shares have changed.
If full details have been given on the return for either of the last two years and there have been no changes please state "No Change".

12. For consistency, it is suggested that particulars should be placed opposite the name of the transferor and not opposite that of the transferee, but the name of the transferee may be inserted in the remarks column opposite the particulars of each transfer.

Bibliography

The Companies Acts are published by Her Majesty's Stationery Office, and are available by post or from HMSO regional bookshops.

The following loose-leaf publications are available from Croner Publications Ltd, Croner House London Road, Kingston upon Thames, Surrey KT2 6SR:

Buying and Selling Law
Guide to Corporation Tax
Management Information Manual
Reference Book for the Self-Employed and Small Business
Reference Book for VAT

Kogan Page publish an extensive list of books for small companies; those particularly useful to the company secretary are likely to be:

The Business Guide to Effective Writing, J A Fletcher and D F Gowing, 1987, published in Association with the Institute of Chartered Accountants in England and Wales
The Cash Collection Action Kit, Philip Gegan and Jane Harrison, 1990
Controlling Cash Flow, David H Bangs, 1989
The European Community Fact Book, Alex Roney, published in association with the London Chamber of Commerce, 1989
Forming a Limited Company, Patricia Clayton, 1990
Law for the Small Business: The Daily Telegraph Guide, 7th edition, Patricia Clayton, 1991
Mastering Business Information Technology, Bob Rothenburg, John Weston and Laurence Pyzer, published in association with *The Daily Telegraph*, 1989
The Stoy Hayward Business Tax Guide, Mavis Seymour and Stephen Saye, annual
Successful Big Business Strategies for Small Firms, Roger Bennett, 1990

Index

Accounting reference date 37, 53
Accounts 37, 68, 69
Agenda 41
Allotment of shares 53, 86
Alteration of Memorandum and
    Articles 83
Annual General Meeting 56, 58,
    63, 64, 68, 69
Annual Return 63, 72
Articles of Association 17, 19, 83
Attendance book 46
Auditor 38, 53, 68, 69, 92

Balance sheet 68
Bank account 39
Bankers 39, 53
Board meetings 40, 55
Business name 37
Business, purchase of 16, 42

Capital 19, 86
Capital duty 89
Certificate of Incorporation 13,
    16, 17
Chairman 22, 43
Change of address 78
Change of auditor 92
Change of name (company) 83
Change of name (shareholders) 78
Charges 20, 81

Circulated resolutions 47
Company:
    definition 10, 65
    formation 15
    purchase 15
Contracts of service 29

Debentures 54, 80
Department of Trade and
    Industry 13
Directors 12, 19, 22, 80
    appointments 23, 51, 80
    disqualification 23, 30
    duties 24, 27
    election 65
    fees 29
    first 17, 21, 23
    interests 27, 28, 46, 63
    liabilities 13
    loans 30
    National Insurance 29
    other directorships 28
    powers 13, 18, 24
    Report 64
    responsibilities 13, 18, 24, 27
    rotation 23, 65
    salaries 29
    termination 91
Directors and Officers Liability
    Insurance 27

112 *Be Your Own Company Secretary*

Disqualification of directors 23
Dividends 63, 78, 80
Documents:
 custody 32
 sealing 85
 search 13
Dormant companies 68
Duties of directors 24
Duties of secretary 31

Elective Resolution 57
Executive directors 22
Extraordinary General Meetings 56, 58
Extraordinary Resolution 60

Fees, directors' 29
Final dividend 81
Financial year 37
Forms, statutory 17, 54, 97
Fraud 30

General meetings 56, 61
Guarantee 10

Income tax 29
Incorporation 11
Increase of capital 86
Insolvency 30
Issue of shares 86
Interim dividend 81

Joint shareholdings 76

Leases 12
Letterheads 36
Letters of Request 75
Limited liability 12, 18
 advantages 12
Liquidation 11, 96
Loan stocks 80
Loans to directors 27, 30
Looseleaf minute book 49
Lost certificates 78
Lost dividend warrants 78

Marriages 78
Meetings 19, 40
 agenda 41
 board 40, 55
 general 40, 56, 69
 minutes 17, 20, 42, 46, 48, 70
 notice 41, 69
 procedure 46, 61
 quorum 42
Members 11, 20
 voting 43
Memorandum of Association 17, 18, 60, 83
Minutes 17, 20, 42, 46, 48
Mortgages 20

Name 16, 35, 83
 acceptability 16
 business 37
National Insurance 29
Nominee shareholdings 93
Non-executive directors 22
Northern Ireland 14
Notice of meetings 41, 61, 69
Numbering of minutes 49

Objects clause 18, 83
Office, Registered 18, 33
Off-the-shelf company 15
Ordinary resolutions 57, 58
Ownership, transfer of 12

Parent company 93
Penalties 32
Poll 60
Powers of directors 24
Pre-emptive rights 90
Preference shares 54, 80
Private company:
 advantages 12
 definition 11
 taxing of 12
Property transactions 27
Proxy 60, 69

Public company, definition 11
Purchase of a business 16, 42

Quorum 42

Register of Charges 81
Register of Shareholders 73
Registered office 18, 33, 52
Registrar of Companies 13
    address 13
    Northern Ireland 14
    Scotland 14
Registration of charges 81
Report of Directors 63, 64
Resolutions 47, 57, 58, 70
Responsibility of directors 13,
    18, 24, 27
Rotation of directors 23, 65

Salaries, directors 29
Seal 17, 20, 37, 85
Secretary 9
    appointment 19, 30, 51, 80
    authority 31
    duties 31
Service contracts 29
Share certificates 17, 20
Shareholders 11
Shares 11, 16, 73, 74
    allotment 53, 86
Share transfer forms 17, 20, 34,
    73
Signature of minutes 50
'Small' company 65

Small estates 76
Special business 70
    notice 69, 91
    Resolution 57, 58
Stationery 35, 36
Statutory books 9, 17, 20, 51, 54
Statutory forms 17
Statutory returns 51, 56
Stock Exchange 11
Striking-off 96
Subscribers 32
Subsidiary company 93

Table A 20
Tax 12
    credit 81
    voucher 78, 81
Termination of director's
    appointment 91
Termination of company 96
Time limits 63, 69, 72
Trade and Industry, Department
    of 13
Transfer of shares 35, 51, 73
Transmission of shares 74
Trust, Declaration of 95

Ultra vires transactions 18

Votes at meetings 43, 60
    casting 44

Waiver of notice 62
Warranties 17, 20